A Straightforward Guide to Probate and the Law

Julie Peters

www.straightforwardco.co.uk

D0308891

British Cataloguing in Publication Data. A catalogue record is available for this book from the British library.

ISBN 9781847161994

Printed by The Berfort Press
Cover design by Bookworks Islington

Whilst every effort has been taken to ensure that the information in this book is accurate at the time of going to press, the author and publisher recognise that the information can become out of date. This is particularly relevant to legal and tax information. The book is therefore sold on the understanding that no responsibility for errors and omissions is assumed and no responsibility is held for the information held within.

Contents

Introduction

Chapter 3. Initial Steps-The Roles and Responsibilities of Executors Pre-Probate   29

Chapter 5. Post Probate-The Distribution of the Estate 59

Introduction

This brief book outlines the important steps that needed to be taken when acting as an executor or administrator of an estate and also applying for probate and distributing the estate.

Death and dealing with death, particularly of a loved one or one who is very close, is an upsetting experience and needs to be dealt with sensitively. The last thing that most people want to deal with is the estate of the deceased person.

However, it is this aspect of death that causes the most problems in many cases. In a persons life there are many elements such as savings and investments, properties, pensions and other assets that accumulate. In many cases, when a person dies, no will has been left and it is down to friends and families to deal with these assets and to deal with the tax situation that may arise. Of course, life is easier if a will has been left spelling out who are the executors of the estate but even here the aftermath can be complicated.

This book will guide the reader through the five distinct stages: the meaning of probate; the will; actions pre-probate; applying for probate; distributing the estate. Although the stages are quite clear, quite often an individuals tax situation can be complicated. This aspect of probate is outlined in Chapter 4.

The book should prove useful to those who are in the process of dealing with the estate of a deceased person and hopefully make the whole situation clearer and less complicated.

****

Chapter 1

Probate

What is probate?

When a person dies, it is necessary for someone to be appointed, with legal authority, to manage the deceased's financial affairs and wind up his/her estate. In law, the uncompleted financial matters of a deceased are known as 'the estate' and the person who is given the legal authority to wind up the estate is called the legal personal representative. After the application for probate, the document which proves the legal authority of the personal representative is called the grant of representation to an estate.

Where to get a grant of representation to an estate

Grants of representation to an estate are obtained from an office of the High Court known as the Probate Registry. The process of obtaining the grant is commonly known as 'probate'.

If someone leaves a will but dies without appointing an executor to carry out the terms of that will, or if the executors who are appointed by the will are unable or unwilling to carry out the duties of an executor, then the grant of representation obtained from the probate registry to prove that the will is a valid one and to authorize the person who obtains it to carry out its terms is called 'letters of administration with the will annexed'. If someone dies without making a will, that person dies intestate and the grant of representation obtained from the probate registry to authorize someone to wind up the estate is called 'letters of administration of the estate'. Those who obtain letters of administration are known as administrators of the estate. The main difference between the executor appointed under the will and the administrator of an estate are that an executors powers are given by the will and are more or less immediate whereas the administrators powers cannot be exercised until the Registry has appointed the administrator.

Essentially, probate and letters of administration can be seen as title documents to the assets of the deceased person's estate. However, there are a few assets where they are not required and can be dispensed with. These include what are known as nominated assets, jointly owned assets owned as joint tenants, estates of small value and estates which consist entirely of personal effects and/or personal currency. There may however still be a requirement to deal with HMRC in relation to inheritance tax. If in doubt contact the HMRC helpline 0845 3020900.

Property held jointly

Assets owned jointly are those that are not held in the sole name of the deceased. In English law, there are two ways of owning property jointly, either as joint tenants or tenants in common. In this sense, the word tenant doesn't mean tenant in the sense of landlord and tenant but is used universally in relationship to ownership of property.

If property is held as joint tenants the law clearly states that on the death of one of the owners, that person's share of the property does not become part of his estate (except for the purposes of Inheritance tax), it is inherited by the surviving joint owners, regardless of what is contained within the will. However, if property is held as tenants in common, the law states that on the death of one owner that persons share of the jointly owned property does become part of his or her estate.

The line between jointly owned property and property held as tenants in common is fine. However, there are a few obvious indicators. Usually, if bank or building society accounts are held jointly, along with stock and shares, they are considered joint tenancies. However, there has to be evidence of equal ownership of property. Any evidence to the contrary such as unequal payments, or sharing of rents, dividends etc, can mean tenancy in common.

Value of the estate
Estates valued under £15,000 gross

If the value of an estate before deducting the cost of the funeral and any debts left by the deceased is under £15,000, it is usually worth contacting organizations such as banks or building societies holding assets, to request that they make payment to the personal representative without going through the formalities of obtaining a grant of representation. They may or may not co-operate but it is worth contacting them. If the amounts involved are low then banks or building societies will co-operate on sight of a valid original will or if there is no will they will deal with the next of kin and a solicitor.

Obtaining a grant of representation and letters of administration

There are a number of main steps involved in obtaining probate or letters of administration with the will annexed or letters of administration and then administering the estate:

1. Obtaining the information necessary to fill out the paperwork to obtain the grant of representation.

2. Preparing the documentation and then lodging the documentation to obtain an inheritance tax assessment and the issue of the grant of representation.

3. Registering the grant in connection with the various assets and giving instructions as to how they are to be dealt with and collecting what is due to the estate.

Following the completion of the three main steps above there are a further three steps:

1. Finalise the income and Capital gains tax positions

2. Pay off the debts and discharge the liabilities of the estate.

3. Distribute the remaining assets of the estate to the beneficiaries.

Dealing with the estate yourself or employing a solicitor

There are obvious advantages to using a solicitor. These are that solicitors are trained in law and can usually give sound guidance. They are usually necessary when it comes to complicated wills. They will take a lot of the work away from the executor which can be very helpful. They also have insurance to cover themselves against negligence. The obvious disadvantages can be the cost. Solicitors charge anything from between £150-250 per hour. In addition, a percentage charge can be made depending on the value of the estate. This is usually between 1-2% of the estate depending on value. If you intend to use a solicitor make sure you are fully acquainted with the costs before you instruct them to act.

Problems with personal representatives

In some cases, a will can specify an executor but that person is unwilling to act. Generally speaking, there is no legal obligation upon an executor or any other person entitled to apply for a grant of representation to apply for one. A person can give up their right to apply by signing a document to that effect, but this document is not binding until it is lodged with a probate registry. When it has been lodged with a Registry he or she cannot then change their mind unless permitted by the court, which is rare. The only person who cannot refuse to take out a grant of representation is an executor of a will who has 'intermeddled' with an estate, which means someone who has already done something which shows an intention to act as executor or apply for a grant of probate.

Removing someone unsuitable to act

If a person who has already taken out a grant of representation to an estate behaves in a manner which is considered improper in relation to the estate or proves unsuitable in some other way, it is then usually possible to commence proceedings in a court to ask that he or she be removed from the position of personal representative and someone else replace him.

Stopping an application for a grant

If someone who is claiming an interest in an estate feels that an application has been made which should not be issued and he or she wants to make their views known to the registry, he or she can give notice to the registry that they wish to be heard before a grant is made. This notice, which is called a caveat, must be in writing and signed by the person issuing the notice. This caveat will last for six months and while it is in force no grant of representation, other than one limited to the below can be made:

- the administration of an estate until the conclusion of litigation currently taking place in the Chancery Division of the High Court in relation to the estate
- the preservation of an estate which will be endangered by delay in administering it.

****

Chapter 2

The will

Who can wind up an estate?

To answer this question we need to go right back to the will, or the existence of a will or otherwise. Who will be entitled to wind up the estate depends on whether or not the deceased has left a valid will or codicil appointing an executor who is still living and prepared to act as an executor. A codicil is a document separate from the will but which is similarly signed and completed and annexed to the will and adds to or amends the will.

The existence of a will

There are several scenarios to consider here. If it is believed widely that the deceased person has made a will but the will cannot be found it may well have been lodged for safe keeping with the deceased's solicitor, bank or other person such as the accountant. If all enquiries draw a blank then enquiries can be made to the Record Keeper's Department at Principal Probate Registry, which is situated at First Avenue House, 42-49 High Holborn, London WC1V 6NP Telephone 0207 947 7000. Wills can be deposited here for safe keeping. The Registry maintains an index of wills which is searched every time a grant of representation application is made. There are several websites in existence where it is possible to check the existence of a will, one such is www.1st.locate.co.uk and also a separate website where wills deposited with solicitors may be searched which is www.certainty.co.uk. Only professional lawyers can search the latter site.

If the will cannot be located it is sometimes possible to prove a will by a copy or by a reconstructed will if the original has been accidentally destroyed or lost. Obviously the evidence must be solid here in order to prove the authenticity of the will.

Is the will a valid document?

If a will is found then certain facts must be considered, such as whether the deceased person had the necessary legal capacity to make a will, whether the requisite formalities were complied with when the will was made, whether the will is valid or whether it has been revoked and to what property the will relates.

Capacity to make a will

For a will to be valid in this respect the person making the will (testator) must have the required degree of understanding to enter into the formation of a will. In other words, was that person of a sound mind? The Mental Capacity Act 2005 contains a code of practice to help judges and others decide whether a person is of a sound mind. However, it is still the usual practice for the mental

18

capacity to make a will to be decided by Common Law principles. Under common law, to have testamentary capacity, in addition to being over the age of 18 (unless a seaman at sea or in the armed forces and on active military service), a testator must:

- be able to understand what making a will means
- be capable of having a rough idea of what he or she has to leave
- be aware of those who will benefit under the will
- understand, in broad terms the effect of the will without his or her decisions being affected by mental disorder.

A testator will be assumed to have testamentary capacity unless it is proved otherwise, and that the provisions of the will are not irrational to a degree that they don't make sense. As long as the person making the will was sane at the time of making it then the will should not be invalid if the testator becomes totally insane after making it.

The making of a valid will

Wills created outside England and Wales

If a will was made outside England and Wales then it will be valid under English law if it was made:

- in accordance with the laws of the country where it was made
- in accordance with the formalities required by the country where, at the time the will was made or at death, the Testator was domiciled or had his habitual residence or of which he was a national.

A will that was made on a ship or an aircraft is treated as validly completed if it was created in accordance with the law of the country with which the ship or aircraft has the closet connection, i.e. British Airways connected to Britain and so on.

Wills which contain stipulations concerning property abroad

If the will deals with immoveable property such as a holiday home, it will be valid under English law if it complies with the formalities of the country in which it was made.

When drafting a will that deals with overseas property (any property) then it is necessary to consider the foreign law relating to property and the making of wills, even if the will was made in the United Kingdom. Some countries, such as France, are very different to the UK in their laws of inheritance. It will be necessary, if leaving property that is situated abroad to obtain advice from a lawyer who specializes in the law of that particular country.

Wills made by a member of the armed forces engaged in actual military service or a seaman at sea

There are very different laws relating to the above. If the will was made by a member of the armed forces engaged in actual military service or a seaman at sea then none of the usual formalities are required to be followed to make, or revoke, a will. These wills can be made irrespective of age, do not have to be in writing, can be made orally provided that the intention is that the conversation shall have testamentary effect. If the will is written, it does not have to be witnessed, and the will is not revoked by lapse of time or a return to civilian life (or in the case of a seaman, to land).

Wills made in England and Wales

If a will made in England or Wales (other than servicemen as discussed above) is to be seen as a valid will, then certain formalities have to be complied with:

- The will must be in writing. Any form of writing is valid, but it must be in writing.
- The will must have been signed and witnessed. To date, electronic signatures are not accepted. The person signing the will can be someone at the testator's request.
- The will must be witnessed by two or more people who are present at the same time. The witnesses must be of age and mentally capable of witnessing a

21

will. Each witness must have signed the will and either signed or acknowledged his signature in the testators presence.

- It must be apparent that the testator intended to give effect to the will by signing it. In practice the signatures of all concerned will be entered at the end of the will.

The revoking of wills

Those engaged in actual military service and seamen at sea can revoke a will at any age, orally and without formalities.

Revocation by marriage or civil partnership

If a person marries or remarries or goes through a civil partnership ceremony after the date of making a will, the will is revoked, unless the will is made with that particular marriage or civil partnership in mind and was intended to remain in force after the event.

Any appointment of property made by will in the exercise of a power of appointment that the testator has will not be revoked if he subsequently enters into a civil partnership (unless the property would form part of his estate if he had not made the appointment).

Revocation by destruction with intention to revoke

A will is revoked if it was destroyed by a testator or by another person at his request and in his presence. In either case, the testator must have intended that the will should be revoked.

However, central to this is the fact that for the whole will to be revoked then this should be apparent and obvious. If the will was only partially destroyed or obliterated for example by tearing a piece out, then this will not revoke the whole will.

The creation of a new will, or revocation by codicil

A new will, or a codicil which contains a clause which states that any previous will is revoked will be effective. If there is a later will containing no revocation clause but which contains provisions inconsistent with a previous will, the provisions of the earlier will which are inconsistent with the new provisions are considered to be revoked. However, all other provisions of the earlier will are effective.

Alterations and obliterations to a will

Alterations, obliterations or insertions in a will or codicil are of no effect if not signed and witnessed in the same way as the whole will.

The effect of divorce or annulment of marriage or dissolution of a civil partnership on a will

Dissolution of any of the above does not invalidate a will, but a decree absolute (not a decree nisi) makes any provisions in a will appointing a spouse or a civil partner as a trustee or executor, or conferring powers of appointment on the spouse or civil partner, invalid. The effect is as if the former spouse or civil partner had died on the day that the decree became absolute.

In the same way, a decree absolute makes any bequest in the will to the spouse or civil partner take effect as if the former spouse or civil partner had died on the same day the decree becomes absolute, leaving bequests in the remainder of the will valid. Usually the bequest will become part of the residue of the estate and be inherited by the residuary beneficiaries, but if the bequest is of the entire estate or of a share of the residue of the estate, it will be treated as not having been disposed of by the will and will be inherited on death according to the laws of intestacy.

Valid wills appointing an under-age executor

If the deceased person has left a valid will or codicil that is relevant to property in England or Wales, the people with the first right to deal with or administer the estate are the executors appointed by the will or codicil. However, if the person appointed is under the age of 18, he or she cannot act although the High Court can appoint the parents or a guardian or other person to act until he or she becomes of age.

Executors who do not wish to act or who wish to delay acting

Even though a person has been named in a will as an executor he or she is not obliged to do so and can sign a form of renunciation giving up the right to the executorship providing that this is done before any rights of executor are exercised. If one appointed executor renounces the right then the other appointed executor can proceed to obtain a grant of probate solely.

An executor who renounces executorship should pass all forms signed to the co-executor(s) or if no other executor is prepared to prove the will then to the person entitled to letters of administration of the estate with the will annexed. An executor who wishes to renounce his right to probate but who cannot find his co-executor or the next person in line to prove the will or entitled to letters of administration of the estate can discharge himself and obtain a receipt by lodging the appropriate documentation such as the form of renunciation at any district probate registry.

If a person wishes to delay his power to act, for whatever reason, allowing the other executors to go ahead, he can reserve the power to prove the will till a later date. This again is done by lodging the appropriate documentation at the probate registry.

If no suitable executor is appointed

If an executor is considered to be unsuitable to act, a court can be requested to remove that person from office and appoint someone else in place. In exercising discretion to appoint or remove personal representatives the court will attach importance to the wishes of the beneficiaries.

If all the executors are unable or unwilling to act, or if the will or codicil has not given anyone the position of executor, or if a court removes the only remaining executor, member of the below groups of people are entitled to apply for a grant of letters of administration with the will annexed:

1. Those entitled (on trust for any other person) to that part of the estate which remains after taking out any specific gifts or legacies made by the will (residue of the estate).
2. Those entitled to the residue of the estate.
3. If the residue is not fully disposed of then those entitled to the part left.
4. The personal representatives of the above (3).
5. Any legatee or creditor of the deceased.
6. The personal representatives of the above (5).

Only when there is no member of a group who is willing to take out a grant is a member of the next group considered.

If there is no valid will

In many cases, unfortunately, there is no valid will and complications arise. If there is no valid will, the following are entitled to wind up the estate:

- Husband or wife or registered civil partner.
- Sons or daughters or their descendants.
- Parents.
- Brothers or sisters of the whole blood, or their descendants.
- Brothers or sisters of the half blood, or their descendants.
- Grandparents.
- Uncles and aunts of the whole blood or descendants.
- Uncles or aunts of the half blood or their descendants.
- The Crown.
- Creditors of the deceased.

Only blood or adoptive relationships count, not step relations.

The number of personal representatives

Not more than four people can obtain grant of representation from a probate registry to act at the same time, even if a will is complex and appoints separate executors for different parts of the estate, such as literary executors, general executors etc.

In the case of letters of administration, the grant is usually given to the first of those equally entitled to apply, but if there is a dispute between them as to whom the grant should be given, the registry will favour those it considers are the most likely the estate the most effectively (to the best advantage of the beneficiaries and the creditors).

****

Chapter 3

Initial Steps after Death-The Role and Responsibilities of Executors Pre-Probate

The formalities

Relatives or friends of the deceased will take on the task of dealing with the necessary formalities after death. In the first instance, notwithstanding where the person dies, a doctor must provide relatives with a certificate stating the cause of death. This certificate is then lodged at the Registry of Births Deaths and Marriages within five days of the issue. The registrar will need to know full details of the death and will also ask for any other certificates such as marriage and birth. The person who registers the death is known as the 'informant'.

If the doctor states that the cause of death is uncertain, then the arrangements are rather more complex. The death will first be reported to the coroner, who usually orders a post-mortem. If it shows that the cause of death was natural, the coroner then authorises the burial or cremation. In these cases, you will be issued with a death certificate by the Registrar and a second certificate permitting the undertaker to arrange burial or cremation.

Except in rare cases, for example violent death when the coroner orders an inquest to be held, it will now be time to organise the funeral. It will be necessary at this point to check the will or if there is no will, to find out about the arrangements for administering the estate.

If the death occurred when the deceased was abroad and it was registered with the British Consulate copies of the death certificate can be obtained from the consulate, or the Overseas Registration Section, General Register Office, Smedleys Hydro, Trafalgar Road, Birkdale, Southport PR8 2HH.

Funeral arrangements

Search for any document which may indicate the wishes of the deceased in relation to their funeral. Muslims and Orthodox Jews are usually buried and Hindus are cremated. Sikhs request cremation and that their ashes are scattered in a river or the sea. Non-Orthodox Jews sometimes request cremation and some Christians prefer burial and others cremation. If a 'Green' funeral is required the natural death centre can supply further information. In practice, the family usually arranges the funeral.

If there is a will in existence, it may well contain details concerning the desired funeral arrangements of the deceased. If there are no clear instructions the executors of the will usually make appropriate arrangements. The executor will become legally liable to pay costs of the funeral.

Where the deceased dies intestate, the 'administrators' of the estate will instruct the undertaker and assume responsibility for payments. In some cases, it may be clear that the deceased does not have enough assets to cover the funeral. If this is the case then investigations need to take place, including the possibility of a one-off funeral grant to cover costs. Once financial details have been settled it is advisable to put a notice in the deaths column of one or more papers to bring the funeral to the attention of relatives.

The responsibilities of executors

Executors and administrators of estates have very important responsibilities. In the first instance they are responsible for ensuring that the assets of the estate are paid to the correct beneficiaries of the will and also for ensuring that all debts are paid before distribution.

If this aspect of administration is mismanaged then the executor or administrator will be held, or could be held, liable for any debts. In order to ensure that they are protected then executors or administrators should advertise in the London Gazette – which is a newspaper for formal notices of any kind, and also a local paper together with requests that creditors should submit their claims by a date which must be at least two months after the advertisement. Private individuals will usually have to produce a copy of probate before their advertisement is accepted for publication.

See sample letters to the London Gazette and local newspapers in Appendix one.

The executor's initial steps

If you are the executor of a valid will (or if you are the administrator if there is no will) you can now begin the task of administering the estate.

It will be essential to ensure that the basic elements are dealt with such as informing utilities, arranging for termination of certain insurance policies and discharge of liabilities of others such as life insurance. Arrangements will need to be made for any pets and post redirected. Valuables that can be stolen should be removed from the building for safekeeping. All licences, such as television licences, car tax and any other necessary licences should be returned and refunds obtained. Arrangements should be made with the post office to redirect mail. Anyone else with a connection to the deceased who may be receiving a benefit, or, for example, may be renting a property from the deceased, has to be notified. If there are tenants then all future rents should be paid to the executor of proposed administrator of the estate. These are the basic essential lifestyle elements before you make an application for probate.

The value of the estate

Before you can apply for probate of the will, you have to find out the extent and value of the assets and liabilities of the estate. You will need to have access to all records of assets, such as insurance policies and bank accounts. The ease with which you can establish a total value will depend on how organised the deceased was. If the deceased was a taxpayer it is advisable to approach the local tax office for a copy of his or her last tax return, sending a copy of the will to prove your status as an executor.

Once you have collated all proof of assets including property you will need to arrive at a total value. The following will provide a pointer for establishing value:

Bank accounts
Interest-bearing accounts and joint bank accounts

When you have found out details of these accounts you should ask for details of balance and accrued interest at the time of death. This is needed for the tax return you will have to complete on behalf of the deceased estate.

These types of accounts can be problematic. If the joint holders are husband and wife, the account will pass automatically to the survivor. In other cases you will need to establish the intentions of the joint owners or the contribution of each to the joint account. This is because the amount contributed by the deceased forms part of the estate for tax purposes (except where a written agreement confirms that the money in the account passes automatically to the survivor). In the case of business partnership accounts, you need a set of final trading accounts to the date of death and should contact the surviving partner.

See example letters to banks and building society in appendix one.

National Savings

These may take the form of National Savings Certificates, National Savings Investment Accounts or Premium Bonds. A claim form for repayment should be obtained, usually from the post office and sent to the appropriate department for National Savings together with a copy of the probate when you have it.

Building societies

You would approach a building society in the same way as a bank, asking for a balance and interest to date. You should also ask for a claim form for payment.

Life insurance

You should write to insurance companies stating the date of death and the policy number and enclose a copy of the death certificate. Once probate has been obtained submit your claim form for monies owed. In many cases, policies are held on trust and will not form part of an estate. Insurance companies will, on production of the death certificate, make payment direct to the beneficiaries.

Stock and shares

You should make arrangements to forward a list of stocks and shares held by the deceased to a bank or stockbroker. In the case of ISA's you should send them to the plan manger and ask for a valuation. Ask for transfer forms for all shareholdings.

You may decide to value the stocks and shares yourself. If this is the case, you will need a copy of the official Stock Exchange Daily Official List for the day on which the deceased died. The valuation figure is calculated by adding 25% of the difference between the selling and buying prices. If the death took place at the weekend you can choose either the Monday or Friday Valuation. However, if the executors sell any shares at a loss within 12 months, the selling price in all cases can be taken as the value at the date of death.

If you cannot locate all of the share certificates, you may be able to find dividend counterfoils or tax vouchers among the papers of the deceased which will enable you to check the number of shares held in the company. If you cannot find share certificates, write to the Registrar of the company. Name of Registrars are given in the Register of Registrars held in the local library. The same approach can be made if the deceased holds unit trusts. In the case of private companies where no value of shares is published, you may sometimes be able to obtain a valuation from the secretary of the company. In the case of a family company it will usually be necessary to have the value determined by a private accountant.

See sample letter in Appendix one.

The employer

If the deceased was employed, then it will be necessary to send a letter to the employer informing them of the death and also requesting details of any salaries owed, pension companies etc.

See sample letter in Appendix one.

Pensions

If the deceased was already receiving a pension, you should write to the company operating the scheme in order to find out further details, i.e. is the pension paid up until the time of death, are there any other beneficiaries after death and so on. Pensions vary significantly and it is very important that accurate information is obtained.

See sample letter in Appendix one.

State benefits

If the deceased was in receipt of an old age pension, notice of the death should be given to the Department of Work and Pensions, so that any adjustments can be made. In the case of married men, the agency will make arrangements to begin to pay widows pension.

Businesses

The valuation of a business on the death of one of the partners is complicated and depends upon the nature of the business, the way in which the accounts are prepared and the extent of the assets held by the business.

The surviving partner/s should make available a set of partnership accounts to the date of death and help you to determine the correct valuation for the deceased share.

Farms

If the deceased had an interest in a farm, any type of farm you should seek advice of a more specialist agricultural valuer.

Residential property

If the estate is below the inheritance tax threshold, you may be able to estimate the value of the property by looking at similar properties in estate agents windows. You may also wish to obtain a professional valuation. If the estate reaches the inheritance tax threshold or is close to it, the figure is checked by the District Valuer. If the property is sold within four years of death for less than the probate valuation, and providing the sellers are executors and not beneficiaries, the sale price may be substituted for the original valuation.

In the case of joint properties, the value of the person who has died forms part of the estate for tax purposes. However, if the share passes to the spouse, the 'surviving spouse exemption' applies. This means that there is no inheritance tax to pay, even if the estate exceeds the inheritance tax threshold.

If there is a mortgage on the property at the date of death, the amount of the debt must be found by writing to the bank or building society. The value of the house is reduced by this amount.

Where the deceased has left residential property as a specific item, the will may either say that the property is to be transferred to the beneficiary free from any mortgage or that it is subject to a mortgage, The Administration of Estates Act provides that a person who is bequeathed a mortgaged property is responsible repaying the mortgage unless the will sets out a contrary intention.

Other property and buildings

If the deceased owned commercial property, the executor has to determine whether this was a business asset or whether it is an investment property unconnected with any business. If this is the case a separate valuation will be needed.

Personal possessions

Although it is not always necessary to obtain professional valuations for household goods, estimated values are examined very carefully by the District Valuer if the estate is large enough to attract inheritance tax. The way household goods are dealt with will depend entirely on their value. In certain cases, with items such as painting and jewellery then an auction may be appropriate.

Income tax

It is very unlikely that, before you make your application for probate, you will be in a position to calculate the income tax owed on an estate. As the administration of the estate gathers momentum then you will amass enough information to start forming a picture of the value and thus the tax liabilities.

See sample letter in Appendix one.

Chapter 4

Making the Application for Probate

Applying for Probate

Probate represents the official proof the validity of a will and is granted by the court on production by the executors of the estate of the necessary documents. Only when probate is obtained are executors free to administer and distribute the estate.

If the value of the estate is under £5000 in total, it may be possible to administer the estate without obtaining probate. Generally, if the estate is worth more than £5000, you will have to apply for probate of the will or letters of administration. There are a number of reasons for this:

- Banks, building societies and National Savings are governed by the Administration of Estates (Small payments) Act 1965. This only allows them to refund individual accounts up to £5000 without production of probate.
- You cannot sell stocks, shares or land from an estate without probate, except in the case of land held in names of joint tenants where this passes on after death
- If the administration is disputed or if a person intends to make a claim as a dependant or member of the family, his

or her claim is 'statute barred' six months after the grant of probate. The right to take action remains open if the estate is administered without probate

- A lay executor who managed to call in the assets of an estate without probate might miss the obligation to report matters to HMRC for inheritance tax purposes, especially where a substantial gift had been made in the seven years prior to the death.

Letters of administration

If someone dies intestate (without making a will) the rules of intestacy laid down by Act of Parliament will apply. An administrator must apply for letters of administration for exactly the same reasons as the executor applies for probate. The grant of letters of administration will be made to the first applicant.

If a will deals with part only but not all of the administration (for example where the will defines who receives what but does not name an executor) the person entitled to apply for letters of administration make the application to the Registrar attaching the will at the same time. The applicant is granted 'Letters of administration with will attached'.

Applying for letters of administration

The following demonstrates the order of those entitled to apply:
- The surviving spouse (not unmarried partner)

- The children or their descendants (once over 18)
- If there are no children or descendants of those children who are able to apply, the parents of the deceased can apply
- Brothers and sisters 'of the half blood'
- Grandparents
- Aunts and uncles of the whole blood
- Aunts and uncles of the half blood
- The Crown (or Duchy of Lancaster or Duchy of Cornwall) if there are no blood relations.

Where the estate is insolvent other creditors have the right to apply.

The Probate Registry – applying for probate

The first step is to obtain the necessary forms from the personal application department of the Principal Probate Registry in London or the local district probate registry. The more straightforward cases can usually be handled by post or by one visit to the probate registry. The executor will complete and send in the forms, they are checked and the amount of probate fees and inheritance tax assessed. The registry officials prepare the official document which the executor then swears, attending personally to do so. The process from submission to swearing usually takes three to four weeks.

Filling in the forms

The necessary forms for applying for probate can be obtained from the probate registry. These are:

- Form PA1 – the probate application form
- Form 1HT 205 – the return of assets and debts

Examples of these forms are shown in Appendix three.

However, see below for more complicated estate returns.

With the forms you will receive other items which serve as guidance to the forms and process:

- 1HT 206 – notes to help you with 1HT 205
- Form PA1 (A) – guidance notes for completing PA1
- Form PA3 – a list of local probate offices
- Form PA4 – a table of fees payable

Form PA1 is fairly uncomplicated. The form is split into white and blue sections with the applicant filling in the white sections. The form will ask which office the applicant wants to attend, details of the deceased, the will and something about you. In cases where more than one executor is involved, the registrar will usually correspond with one executor only. The form also has a space for naming any executors who cannot apply for probate, e.g. because they do not want to or have died since the will was written. If they may apply at a later date, the probate office will send an official 'power reserved letter' which the non-acting executor signs. This is a useful safeguard in case the first executor dies or becomes incapacitated before grant of probate is obtained. You do not have to sign form PA1. At the end of the process, the probate registry will couch the information you supply in legal jargon for the document you are required to sign.

Form PA1 contains a reminder that you have to attach the death certificate, the will and the completed IHT form. If this form demonstrates that the estate exceeds the 'excepted estate' threshold (for inheritance tax purposes) form 1HT 200 will have to be completed.

Procedure for obtaining probate where the tax situation is more complicated

Although the procedure for obtaining a grant of probate, a grant of letters of administration or a grant of letters of administration with will annexed are similar, the procedure concerning inheritance tax accounts is rather more complicated.

There are three types of inheritance tax account, with different forms in each case. They are as follows:

1. If the deceased lived abroad and he or she has few assets in the UK, then form IHT207 will usually be the one to use. In some cases form IHT 400 must be used but form IHT 207 will make this clear.

2. If the deceased was domiciled in the United Kingdom then form IHT 205 is the usual form to use where:

- the gross value of the estate does not exceed the excepted estate limit, which is the inheritance tax threshold (currently £325,000) unless a grant of probate is applied for before 6ᵗʰ of August in the tax year in which the death took place, in which case the excepted estate limit is the inheritance tax limit set for the previous tax year
- the gross value is not more than £1000,000 and there is no tax to pay after taking into account the value of the assets inherited by exempt bodies, such as charities or the deceased's spouse or civil partner, if the deceased and the spouse or civil partner were both born in the United Kingdom and were domiciled here throughout their lives

The gross value of a person's estate is the total value of his assets together with the value of any gifts made by him (a) in the seven years before his death or (b) from which he continued to benefit and upon which he had elected not to pay the pre-owned assets income tax charge or (c) from which he had reserved a benefit.

Form IHT 400 should be used if:

- the deceased was domiciled in the United Kingdom but his estate does not fall within the above classes

- the estate includes an alternatively secured pension, that is, a pension benefit in a pension scheme registered under section 153 of the Finance Act 2004 which has been earmarked to provide benefits for a person over the age of 75 but not used to provide pension benefits or an annuity for him

- the deceased had an unsecured benefit from a pension scheme registered under section 153 of the Finance Act 2004 and he acquired the benefit as a dependent of a person who died aged 75 or over

- the deceased had not taken his full retirement benefits before he died from a personal pension policy or a pension scheme of which he was a member and when he was in poor health, he changed the policy or scheme so as to make a change in or to dispose of the benefits to which he was entitled

- the deceased ever bought an annuity and within seven years of his death paid premiums for a life assurance policy of which the policy monies were not payable to his estate, his spouse or civil partner

- the deceased had a right to benefit from assets held in a trust (other than assets held in a single trust which do not exceed £150,000)

- within seven years of his death the deceased gave up a right to benefit from assets valued at more than £150,000 held in trust

- within seven years of his death the deceased made gifts (other than normal birthday, festive, marriage or civil partnership gifts not exceeding £3000 per year) totaling over £150,000
- the deceased made a gift after 18th March 1986 from which he continued to benefit or in respect of which the person who received the gift did not take full possession of it
- the deceased had made an election that the pre-owned assets income charge should not apply to assets he had previously owned or to the cost of which he had contributed and in either case from which he had continued to benefit
- the deceased lived abroad and form IHT 207 is not appropriate
- the deceased owned or benefited from assets outside the United Kingdom worth more than £100,000
- the estate intends to claim and benefit from any unused nil-rate inheritance tax band of a spouse or civil partner who has died before the deceased (this is done by completing for IHT 402 and returning it with the completed form IHT 400.

Distributing an estate in accordance with the law of intestacy

If someone dies without making a will he is said to die intestate and his estate is inherited according to the law of intestacy. Intestacy law divides relatives into groups or classes according to their blood relationships to the deceased. All members of a given class inherit in equal shares. There is a specific order in which the various classes inherit and if all members of a given class have died before the deceased without leaving issue who survived the deceased, the next class inherits. The words 'child' and 'children' are used to mean a persons immediate dependents (as opposed to grandchildren) and do not include a stepchild or stepchildren, but no distinction is made before legitimate and illegitimate children. Adopted children inherit from their adoptive parents and not from their birth parents.

If those entitled to inherit are under 18, then the inheritance is held in trust for them, until they either reach the age of 18, marry or enter into a registered civil partnership.

To decide who is entitled to inherit, look for the first class and if there is no member of the class who survived the deceased or predeceased him look for those in the next class.

The law of intestacy

If there is a lawful spouse or civil partner and the deceased died **leaving children** then the spouse receives the first £250,000 for dates of death after February 1st 2009 in respect of assets solely in the deceased's name plus a life interest in half of the remaining capital, children receive half remaining capital, then on the death of the spouse/civil partner the children receive the remaining capital.

If there is a **lawful spouse/civil partner** and the deceased died **leaving no children**, the spouse receives the first £450,000 for dates of death after February 1st 2009 in respect of assets solely in the deceased's name plus half of the remaining capital. The remaining half of the capital goes to parent(s) if any, if not then to brother/sister of whole blood and issue of predeceased brother/sister of the whole blood.

If there are children, but no spouse or civil partner, everything goes to the children in equal shares.

If there are parent(s) but no spouse or civil partner or children then everything goes to parents in equal shares.

If there are brothers or sisters, but no spouse or civil partner, or children or parents everything goes to brothers and sisters of the whole blood equally.
If there are no brothers or sisters of the whole blood, then all goes to brothers and sisters of the half blood equally.

If there are grandparents, but no spouse or civil partner, or children or parents, or brothers and sisters everything goes to the grandparents equally.

If there are uncles and aunts, but no spouse or civil partner, or children or parents, or brothers or sisters or grandparents, then everything goes to uncles and aunts of the whole blood equally.

If there are no uncles and aunts of the whole blood, then all goes to uncles and aunts of the half blood equally.

If there is no spouse or civil partner and no relatives in any of the categories shown above then everything goes to the Crown.

Notes

A spouse is a person who was legally married to the deceased when he or she died.

A civil partner is someone who was in a registered civil partnership with the deceased when he or she died. It doesn't include people simply living together as unmarried partners or as common law husband and wife.

The term children includes children born in or out of wedlock and legally adopted children; it also includes adult sons and daughters. It does not, however, include stepchildren.

Brothers and sisters of the whole blood have the same mother and father. Brothers and sisters of the half blood (more commonly referred to as half brothers and sisters) have just one parent in common.

Uncles and aunts of the whole blood are brothers and sisters of the whole blood of the deceased's father or mother.

Uncles and aunts of the half blood are brothers and sisters of the half blood of the deceased's father or mother.

It is important to note that if any of the deceased children die before him, and leave children of their own (that is grandchildren of the deceased) then those grandchildren between them take the share that their mother or father would have taken if he or she had been alive. This also applies to brothers and sisters and uncles and aunts of the deceased who have children – if any of them dies before the deceased, the share that he or she would have had if he or she were still alive, goes to his or her children between them.

The principle applies through successive generations – for example a great grandchild will take a share of the estate if his father and his grandfather (who were respectively the grandson and son of the deceased) both died before the deceased.

It is important to note that if any of the following situations apply to you, or if you are in any doubt whatsoever, you should seek legal advice before distributing the estate of a person who has died without leaving a will:

- The deceased died before 4th of April 1988
- Anyone entitled to a share of the estate is under 18
- Someone died before the deceased and the share he or she would have had goes to his or her children instead
- The spouse/civil partner dies within 28 days of the deceased.

A spouse or civil partner must outlive the deceased by 28 days before they become entitled to any share of the estate.

An ex-wife or civil partner (who was legally divorced from the deceased or whose civil partnership with the deceased was dissolved before the date of death) gets nothing from the estate under the rules of intestacy, but he/she may be able to make a claim under the inheritance (Provision for Family and Dependants) Act 1975, through the courts. Legal advice should be sought if making such a claim.

Anyone who is under 18 (except a spouse or civil partner of the deceased) does not get his or her share of the estate until he or she become 18, or marries under that age. It must be held on trust for him or her until he or she becomes 18 or gets married.

Apart from the spouse or civil partner of the deceased, only blood relatives, and those related by legal adoption, are entitled to share in the estate. Anyone else who is related through marriage and not by blood is not entitled to a share in the estate.

If anyone who is entitled to a share of the estate dies after the deceased but before the estate is distributed, his or her share forms part of his or her own estate and is distributed under the terms of his or her will or intestacy.

Great uncles and great aunts of the deceased (that is brothers and sisters of his or her grandparents) and their children are not entitled to a share in the estate.

Various points concerning distributions of the estate

Children conceived by artificial insemination or in vitro fertilisation

When distributing to those known to have been conceived by artificial insemination or by in vitro fertilisation the following should be borne in mind:

Except for inheritance of titles and land which devolves with titles, if a child is artificially conceived as above:

- In the case of a couple who are married and not judicially separated, the husband is considered to be the father unless it can be proved that he did not consent to the conception
- In the case of treatment provided for a man and woman together, the man is considered to be the father irrespective of whether or not his sperm was used
- The mother is the woman who has carried the child as the result of the placing in her of an embryo or of an egg or sperm.

Although the Human Fertilisation and Embryology (Deceased Fathers) Act 2003 permits a deceased husband or partner to be registered as the father of a child conceived after his death by the use of his sperm, the registration does not give the child any rights of inheritance.

Underage beneficiaries

Unless permitted to do so by the will, neither a person under the age of 18 nor that persons parent or guardian can give a valid receipt for the capital of the bequest (as opposed to the income that it produces) and cannot give a valid discharge for any capital payment made to him. A valid receipt for income produced by a bequest to a person who is under the age of 18 can only be given by the person, or his parent or guardian, if the beneficiary is married or in a registered civil partnership. Accordingly, a personal representative should not make any capital payment to a minor, or an income payment to an unmarried minor who is not in a registered civil partnership unless authorised by the will. The money should be either held on trust until of age or paid into court.

Bankrupts and those of unsound mind

Payments should not be made to a beneficiary who is bankrupt. Similarly, if a bequest has been made to a person who is not believed to be of sound mind, the bequest should not be made to that person personally but to his deputy appointed by the court of protection or to his attorney appointed by an enduring power of attorney made by him before 1st October 2007 or a lasting power of attorney. In the case of both types of power of attorney the powers must have been registered with the Public Guardian and made before the beneficiary lost his sanity.

Beneficiaries who cannot be found

There may be cases where it is difficult to trace a beneficiary, even though every effort may have been made, such as advertising in the local paper or even national papers. If executors do not personally know a beneficiaries address or whereabouts then other exhaustive searches will have to be made, such as the local telephone directory where the beneficiary lives

There are other avenues which can be explored. One is that of the Traceline Team at the Office for National Statistics, tel 01514 714811 www.gro.gov.uk/gro/content they can trace and forward a letter to anyone who is registered with a National Health Service general practitioner in England or Wales if the executor can supply the person's name and date of birth. A fee is payable. Traceline will also inform the executor if the beneficiary has died.

Tracing agencies can be employed, they are costly and should only be used if the sum involved justifies spending significant sums to trace the person.

Sending the forms
If the estate you are administering can be contained on form 1HT 205, you are ready to send in your application. Make sure that

you take photocopies of all material. You should send the
following:

- The will
- The death certificate
- Probate application form PA1
- Short form 1HT 205
- A cheque for the fee

Attach any explanatory letter as necessary. You should then send
the package by registered post. A few weeks later, you will be
invited to review the documents, pay the probate fee and swear
the prescribed oath. Remember to take your file of background
papers.

Probate fees are calculated on the amount of the net estate, as
declared for the purpose of inheritance tax. Fees are payable when
you attend the interview at the registry – see form PA4 for
guidance.

Attendance at the probate registry

When you arrive at the probate registry you will need to examine
the forms that have been prepared for you. You need to satisfy
yourself that all the details are correct. When you have checked all
the details, the commissioner will ask you to sign the original will
and swear the oath, identifying the will as that of the deceased.

The actual process entails you standing up, holding a copy of the New Testament and repeating the words spoken by the commissioner. The words take the form of 'I swear by Almighty God that this is my name and handwriting and that the contents of this my oath are true and that this is the will referred to'. The form of oath is varied depending on religious belief or otherwise.

The commissioner will then sign beneath your signature on the official form and will. The fees are paid and any sealed copies as ordered will be supplied.

Letters of administration

If the deceased has left no will, then the next of kin will apply for a grant of letters of administration instead of probate. The same is the case if a will was left but no executors appointed. In these cases, the grant is called 'letters of administration with will annexed'

When letters of administration are sought, the administrators may in some cases have to provide a guarantee – for example where the beneficiaries are under age or mentally disabled or when the administrator is out of the country. The guarantee is provided by an insurance company at a cost or by individuals who undertake to make good – up to the gross value of the estate – any deficiency caused by the administrators failing in their duties.

Letters of administration may also be taken out by creditors of an estate if executors deliberately do not apply for probate – for instance, if the estate has insufficient assets to pay all creditors and legatees.

The grant of probate

There may be a time lapse of six weeks or more between lodging the probate papers and the meeting at the registry to sign and swear them. After this has happened, however, things move quickly. If there is no inheritance tax to be paid – where the net estate is less than £325,000, or where the deceased property goes to the spouse – the grant of probate (or letters of administration) is issued within a few days. If inheritance tax is due, it takes two to three weeks before the exact amount is calculated and the grant is usually ready about a week later.

The grant of probate is signed by an officer of the probate registry. Attached to the grant of probate is a photocopy of the will. (all original wills are kept at the Principal Probate Registry in London). Each page of your copy of the will carries the impress of the courts official seal. It is accompanied by a note which explains the procedure for collecting and distributing the estate and advises representatives to take legal advice in the event of dispute or other difficulty.

Chapter 5

Post Probate-The Distribution of the Estate

The distribution of the estate of the deceased

Having established probate, it is now time to begin to distribute the estate. Before you can do this, however, it is essential that you understand exactly what the will says. The executor can be sued for payment if the estate is not distributed exactly in accordance with the stipulations in the will. Although this may sound like common sense, some wills may be couched in a particular way, or in a particular jargon and you may need advice on the interpretation.

Specific legacies and bequests

Legacies are, usually, the payment of specific sums of money. Bequests usually mean gifts of goods or cash. 'Devises' means gifts of land or buildings. If the state is not subject to inheritance tax and the legacies and bequests are small, legacies can be paid without further delay and also specific items can be handed over. It is advisable to obtain a receipt from the beneficiary(s) when they receive their gift or legacy.

Transferring property

If a beneficiary has been left a house or other property then any outstanding debts relating to the property, such as a mortgage have to be dealt with. The will usually directs the executors to pay off the mortgage. However, if the will is silent on this point then it will become the responsibility of the beneficiary. It is quite usual that a property is left to another with a mortgage and equity in the property so the beneficiary can continue to pay.

It will be necessary to transfer the property into your own name by contacting the Land Registry. If the property is already registered, as is most property, the process will be straightforward. However, if it is unregistered then you will need to obtain a first registration. At the same time obtain advice about settling the mortgage and also enquire about any arrears of ground rent and other money due if it is a leasehold property. You would probably need to instruct a solicitor to do this as the process can be complicated, particularly if it is leasehold or there are other complications such as joint ownership etc.

Preparation of final accounts

In appendix one, there are samples of letters which need to be sent having received the grant of representation. These letters are usually follow on letters from the pre probate process where you are now claiming assets from banks, building societies, pension funds, employers, stockbrokers and so on.

Having gathered the assets and obtained a good idea of the value you can now begin to prepare final accounts. There is no set form for the final accounts but assets and liabilities must be included, receipts and payments made during the administration and a distribution account of payments to beneficiaries.

It is helpful to include a covering sheet to the accounts, a form of memorandum which will cover the following areas:

- Details of the deceased and date of death, date of probate and names of executors
- A summary of the bequests made in the will
- Particulars of property transfers
- Reference to any valuations which have been included in the accounts

In estates where inheritance tax has been paid, you should prepare one part of the capital account based on the value of the assets at the time of death.

The second part of the account should demonstrate the value of those assets and liabilities at the date they are realised or paid. If the net effect is to reduce the value of the estate, you may be able to claim a refund from the capital taxes office. Conversely you may have increased taxes to pay. In either case you should advise the capital taxes office.

A model set of accounts are shown at the end of the chapter. The capital account shows the value of assets when they are cashed or realised and the debts are the sums actually paid. The income account shows the income received during the administration, less associated expenses. It is convenient to run this account from the date of death to the following 5th of April.

The distribution account shows the capital and income transferred from the respective accounts and how the residue of the estate has been divided. If there is only one beneficiary you should show the final figure. If any items have been taken in kind – such as a car or a piece of furniture – its value is included in the distribution account as both an asset and payment. If you are claiming executor's expenses itemise them and include them in the distribution account.

Where a will exists

When you have completed your accounts, and all outstanding debts and liabilities have been met, you will now be in a position to calculate how much each residuary beneficiary receives according to the specific provisions of the will. In practice, the amount that you have left in the executor's bank account should match the sums to be paid out.

After having ascertained that this is the case, and rectified any errors you should send the accounts to the beneficiaries for their agreement or otherwise. In cases involving inheritance tax, you should contact the capital taxes office and confirm that you have disclosed the full value of the estate. You then apply for a clearance certificate. When you have received this you can make the final distribution to the beneficiaries.

The beneficiaries should be asked to sign an acknowledgement that they agree the accounts and that they agree the amount that they will receive.

Where beneficiaries are deceased or missing

If a beneficiary dies before the death of the testator, the general rule is that the legacy cannot be made. There are a few exceptions to this rule:

- If the will contains a 'substitution' (an alternative to the beneficiary)
- If the gift is made to two people as joint tenants – the survivor being the beneficiary
- If section 33(2) of the Wills Act 1837 applies. This section provides that, if the share of the estate or gift is to a child or other descendant of the testator and the child dies before the testator leaving 'issue' (children and their descendants) they take the share of the gift.

If a beneficiary cannot be located, you must take steps to find that person. These steps must be reasonable. As stated, an advertisement can suffice, as well as contacting relatives and so on.

You can apply to the court for an order giving you permission to distribute the estate on agreed terms You can claim any expenses incurred from the estate.

It is very important, if you cannot find a beneficiary that you take steps to obtain a court order in order to protect yourself from any future problems arising should a beneficiary turn up.

The children's trust under intestacy rules

We saw earlier in the book how an estate is distributed according to the rules of intestacy. When the surviving spouse has children, whatever their age, and the estate is worth more than £125,000, the administrators of the estate must set up a trust to look after the children's share. As trustees, they must invest half the remaining capital in their own names. They notify HMRC of the new trust and submit a Trust Tax return each year. The income from the trust is paid to the spouse. On the death of the spouse, the capital held in the trust account is shared between the children unless they are under 18.

If any of the children die, leaving children of their own, before the death of the intestate or – whichever is the later – second parent, the Statutory Trust rules apply. Under these rules, where a child of the intestate has died leaving children who are 18 or over (or who marry before 18) the children get their parents share. The same applies if the only survivors are grandchildren or even remote descendants.

In some cases, intestacy rules can be rigid and cause hardship. You should always take advice when dealing with distribution of assets in cases that are complicated to resolve.

See overleaf for an example of administration accounts.

Example of Administration Accounts

In the Estate of   Deceased.
Date of death

CAPITAL ACCOUNT
Assets

House Net sales proceeds	£145,000
(value at death £155,000)	
Less mortgage	£95,000
	£50,000
Stocks and shares	£89,000
(value at death £86500)	
Life policy	£7500
Skipton BS deposit	£9000
Interest to date of death	£75
National Savings – Premium bonds	£7000
Arrears of pension	£325
Agreed value of house contents	£3800
Car	£5600
Gross estate	
	£172,300

Less debts and liabilities

Funeral costs	£2000
Gas	£270
Electricity	£25
Administration expenses	£45
Probate fees	£130
Stockbrokers valuation fee	£250
Income tax paid to date of death	£650

Inheritance tax paid on application for probate (N/a) estate less than £240,000

Net Estate carried to distribution account

£168930

For the estate to attract inheritance tax the value would need to be above £240,000. If that is the case, carry on the calculation for inheritance tax by multiplying the residue after £240,000 by 40% which will give you the inheritance tax due.

In the estate of   Deceased

Income account
Dividends received for period from 1st October 2008 to 5th April 2009

Holding	Company	Net dividend
5000 shares	ABC PLC	£1400

4300 shares	Halifax PLC	£560
12000 shares	GKN	£1420
3760 shares	Powergen	£420
Savings accounts final interest		£150

Balance transferred to distribution account

£3950

In the estate of   Deceased

Distribution account

Balance transferred from capital account   £168930

Balance transferred from income account   £3950

£172880

Less payment of legacies

David Peters   £5000

Net residuary estate for distribution   £167880

Mr Frederick Dillon

A one half share represented by

a) House contents   £3800

b) The balance   £80140

Stella Donaldson
One half share represented by the balance   £83940
Total

_____

                                                                £167880

Glossary of terms

Administrator
The person who administers the estate of a person who has died intestate

Bequest
A gift of a particular object or cash as opposed to 'devise' which means land or buildings

Chattels
Personal belongings of the deceased

Child
Referred to in a will or intestacy – child of the deceased including adopted and illegitimate children but, unless specifically included in a will, not stepchildren

Cohabitee
A partner of the deceased who may be able to claim a share of the estate. The term 'common law wife' has no legal force.

Confirmation
The document issued to executors by the sheriff court in Scotland to authorise them to administer the estate

Devise
A gift of house or land

Disposition
A formal conveyancing document in Scotland

Estate
Al the assets and property of the deceased, including houses, cars, investments, money and personal belongings

Executor
The person appointed in the will to administer the estate of a deceased person

Heritable estate
Land and buildings in Scotland

Inheritance tax
The tax which may be payable when the total estate of the deceased person exceeds a set threshold (subject to various exemptions and adjustments)

Intestate
A person who dies without making a will

Issue
Al the descendants of a person, i.e. children, grandchildren, great grandchildren#

Legacy
A gift of money

Minor
A person under 18 years of age

Moveable estate
Property other than land or buildings in Scotland

Next of Kin
The person entitled to the estate when a person dies intestate

Letters of administration
The document issued to administrators by a probate registry to authorise them to administer the estate of an intestate

Personal estate or personalty
Al the investments and belongings of a person apart from land and buildings

Personal representatives
A general term for both administrators and executors

Probate of the will
The document issued to executors by a probate registry in England, Wales and Northern Ireland to authorise them to administer the estate

Probate Registry
The Government office which deals with probate maters. The principal Probate Registry is in London with district registries in cities and some large towns

Real estate or realty
Land and buildings owned by a person

Residue
What is left of the estate to share out after all the debts and specific bequests and legacies have been paid

Specific bequests
Particular items gifted by will

Testator
A person who makes a will

Will
The document in which you say what is to happen to your estate after death

Useful Addresses

Department for National Savings
Glasgow G58 1SB
For enquiries about Capital Bonds, Childrens Bonus Bonds, FIRST Option Bonds, Fixed Rate Savings Bonds, Ordinary Accounts and Investment Accounts.

Department for National Savings
Durham DH99 1NS
Enquiries about deposit bonds, Cash mini-ISA's Savings Certificates, SAYE Contracts and Yearly Plan Agreements

Department for National Savings
Blackpool FY3 9YP
Enquiries about Premium Bonds, Pensioners guaranteed bonds

Tel 0845 964 5000 (Central Helpline)
www.nationalsavings.co.uk

Department of Work and Pensions
Newcastle Benefits Directorate
Cathedral Square
Newcastle Upon Tyne NE1 1EE

For pensions enquiries
0191 152000
www.dss.gov.uk

HM Revenue and Customs Capital Taxes Office
Ferrers House
PO Box 38
Castle Meadow Road
Nottingham NG2 1BB
0115 742400
www.inlandrevenue.gov.org

The Law Society of England and Wales
113 Chancery lane
London WC2A 1PL
0207 242 1222
Public information including solicitors who specialise in wills and probate
www.lawsociety.org.uk

London Gazette
PO Box 7923
London SE1 5ZH
020 7394 4517

Office for the Supervision of Solicitors
Victoria Court
8 Dormer Place
Leamington Spa
Warwickshire CV32 5AE
01926 820082

www.solicitors-online.com
Information on solicitors specialising in wills and probate

The Principal Probate Registry
First Avenue House
42-49 High Holborn
London WC1V 6NP
0845 3020 900
www.courtservice.gov.uk

OYEZ Straker
PO Box 55
7 Spa road
London SE16 3QQ
0207 556 3345

Useful Addresses in Scotland
Accountant of Court
2 Parliament Square
Edinburgh EH1 1RQ
0131 240 6742
www.scotscourts.gov.uk

HMRC Capital Taxes
Meldrum House
15 Drumsheugh Gardens
Edinburgh EH3 7UG
0131 777 4343 (helpline)

www.inlandrevenue.gov.uk (home pages download leaflets free of charge)
www.inlandrevenue.gov.cto.iht.htm (Inheritance tax)

Law Society of Scotland
26 Drumsheugh Gardens
Edinburgh EH3 7YR
0131 226 7411 (Head Office) www.lawscot.org.uk

Registers of Scotland
Customer Service Centre
Erskine House
68 Queen Street
Edinburgh EH2 4NF
0845 607 0161
Or
Registers of Scotland
Customer Service Centre
9 George Square
Glasgow G2 1DY
Tel 0845 6070164
www.ros.gov.uk

Sheriff Clerks Office
Commissary Department
27 Chambers Street
Edinburgh EH1 1LB
0131 225 2525

Appendix 1
Example letters

Sample letter which should accompany the advertisement for creditors and claimants-local newspaper

---

The   Daily Times

Dear Sirs/Madam

In respect of   Deceased

Further to our discussions, please find enclosed an advertisement pursuant to Section 27 of the Trustee Act 1925. Please insert this into your newspaper for one week only.

Yours faithfully

Letter to the London Gazette requesting form for advertising for claimants and creditors.

To: The Manager
the London Gazette
PO Box 7923
London SE1 5ZH

Dear Sir/Madam

Could you please send me a form for completion to enable me to have an advertisement placed in the London Gazette pursuant to section 27 of the Trustees Act 1925. Please let me have a note of any fees payable to you.

Yours faithfully

To The London Gazette enclosing a form for advertisement for claimants and creditors

---

To: The Manager
the London Gazette
PO Box 7923
London SE1 5ZH

Dear Sir/Madam
Re: The Deceased

Please find enclosed an advertisement for claimants and creditors plus office copy of grant of representation for inspection and return, along with a cheque for payment. Please publish the advertisement in the first available issue of the Gazette.

Yours faithfully

Letters to be sent pre-grant of probate

Letters to banks and building societies

The manager
(Bank/Building Society)

Dear Sir/Madam

I am the executor/administrator of the estate of your customer (insert name and address plus account numbers as appropriate). This person passed away on the   and I enclose a registrar's death certificate and a copy of the will (if there is a will).

Please could you let me have any details of accounts, all accounts, which the deceased has with your organisation, particulars of any assets or securities held for safe custody plus any other financial documents which will be relevant in forming a picture of the estate.

Please forward the following in respect of each account held in the deceased's name:

1. balance of account as at the date of death plus any interest owed.

2. Interest accrued to the account between the end of the last financial year and the date of death.

3. Whether the interest is paid gross or net.

4. Whether there are any direct debits or standing orders in respect of each account. please supply particulars.

Any other credit balances on non-interest bearing accounts in the deceased's sole name should be placed on deposit until production of the grant of probate has been given.

Can you let me know your requirements for closing the accounts in the deceased's sole name, and let me have any necessary forms. Please confirm that any accounts held jointly can continue to be operated by the surviving account holder.

Please cancel any standing orders in respect of the accounts and do not meet any further direct debits.

Please send all future communications to me at the above address. please do not hesitate to contact me on the above phone number.

Please find enclosed (passbooks etc).

Yours faithfully

Letter to registrars of companies in respect of stocks and shares

To: The Registrar (Company name address)

Dear Sir/madam

Re: (Deceased) (Company name and share account number etc)

I am the personal representative of   and I enclose a death certificate for your attention. Please register and return.

Can you please confirm the extent of the deceased's holding and let me have the transfer deeds for completion to enable the transfer to beneficiaries when probate is obtained.

Yours faithfully

Letter to Stockbrokers

To: (Company name address)

Dear Sir/madam

I am the personal representative of   and I enclose a death certificate for your attention. Please register and return.

Please let me have a statement of the deceased nominee account with you as at the date of death specifying the deceased holdings and cash position. This is for the purposes of distribution on obtaining probate.

Yours faithfully

Letter to creditors

To: (Insert name and address of creditor)

Dear Sir/Madam

Re: Account number

I am the executor/proposed administrator of the estate of
who died on   and I enclose a death certificate for your
records. Please return original.

Please let me have a final statement detailing the amount claimed.
Please note, in light of the fact that the debtor has died, please
take no enforcement action until the estate is in funds, probate is
granted and distributions made.

All future correspondence re the deceased should be sent to the
above address.

Yours faithfully

Letter to employer

To (employer)
Attention of the payroll department

Deaf Sir/Madam

Re: (Deceased) (Payroll number if known)

I am the executor/administrator of the above estate who died on
        and who was employed by your company as
I enclose a death certificate for your records please return the
original.
Please supply the following:

1. Whether any salary is due to the above and your requirements
for them to be claimed.
2. The gross amount of salary paid in the current financial year
and income tax paid.
3. Whether the above was a member of a pension fund. if so,
please supply details.
4. The name and address of the tax district relevant to the
deceased.
All future communications should be sent to me at the above
address.
Yours faithfully

Letter to HMRC in respect of Income tax

To HM Inspector of Taxes

(Name and Address)

Insert tax reference if known

Dear Sir/Madam

I am the executor/administrator of the estate of (Deceased) who died on   I enclose a death certificate for your records. please copy and return the original.

Please supply me with a copy of the deceased's last tax return and the appropriate forms to enable me to make a return to the date of death and in due course a personal representative's return for the period to the finalisation of the estate.

Please let me have details of any tax outstanding or any repayments due to the deceased and your requirements to enable these matters to be dealt with.

Please address all future communications to me at the above address.
Yours faithfully

Letter to mortgage company

To: The Manager (name and address of company)

Dear Sir/madam

(Mortgage reference address of property mortgaged and name of deceased)

I am the executor/administrator of the above named customer who died on   I enclose a death certificate for you to copy and return the original.

Can you please let me know the capital amount outstanding on the account to the date of death. Please also let me know the amount of interest outstanding at the date of death.

Please let me have details of any endowment policy and the company involved. The grant of representation will be registered with you when it has been granted and I will then let you know the position concerning the mortgage, i.e. whether it is to be paid off or continued in the beneficiaries name.

Until that time, please see that no enforcement action be taken. Please send all correspondence to the above address.
Yours faithfully

Letter to pension fund where pension is already being paid

To: The Secretary
(Name and address)

Dear Sir/madam

Insert details of pension number name etc
I am the executor/administrator of the estate of   who
died on   I enclose a death certificate which should be
copied with the original returned.

Please let me know:

1. Whether there are any arrears of pension due to the estate to
the date of death or any overpaid pension due to be refunded to
the pension fund.
2. Your requirements to enable you to pay any arrears.
3. the gross amount of pension payable in the current tax year,
including sums to the date of death but not yet paid.
4. the amount of tax deducted or which will be deducted from the
current tax years pension.
5. the address and reference number for the relevant tax district.
All communications re the above should now be addressed to me.
Yours faithfully

To pension fund where pension is not yet being paid

The Secretary

(name and address)

Dear Sir/madam

Re: (Deceased) (pension number)

I am the executor/administrator of the estate of   who is a contributor to a pension fund administered by you. The deceased passed away on   and I enclose a death certificate for your records. please return the original.

I understand that the deceased, who was employed by   was a member of your scheme. Please let me know what benefits are due to the deceased's estate and dependants and whether the benefits are subject to inheritance tax. Please send all correspondence concerning the deceased to the above address.
Yours faithfully

Post Grant of Representation

Banks and building societies

To: The Manager
Address

Dear Sir/madam

Name and account number

Further to my recent correspondence to you, please find an office copy grant of probate/letters of administration for your records. please note and return.

I enclose the completed withdrawal forms for your attention.

Please close the account and let me have a remittance for the sum due together with a final statement of account.

Yours faithfully

To registrars in respect of shares and stock (certificated holdings)

To: the registrar
Name and address

Dear Sir/madam

Re: Deceased name and address reference number

I am the personal representative of   and I enclose an office copy of grant of representation for your records and to return. I also enclose the relevant certificates together with the un-cashed (dividend/interest) warrant(s) in respect of the holdings set out below.

Please amend or reissue the warrants in my name so that they can be paid into the estates bank account. Please endorse the certificates so that they can be sold.

Yours faithfully

Stock brokers

To

name and address

Dear Sirs

Re: (name and reference number if known)

I am the personal representative of   and I enclose an
office copy of grant of representation for registration and return in
respect of the deceased's holdings in (name of relevant companies)

Please transfer/sell the holdings as follows (set out details of the
required transfers or sales for each company stating the relevant
number of shares or amount of stock, and name and address of
each transferee if transfers are required).

Yours faithfully

Creditors paying account

To

Name and address

Dear Sirs

Re: My previous communication in respect of

I enclose a cheque in the sum of   in settlement of your
enclosed account. Please send a receipt as soon as possible.

Yours faithfully

Inspector of taxes notifying end of administration period and enclosing final tax return

To: HM Inspector of Taxes

Name and address

tax reference

Dear Sir/madam

Re: (Deceased details)

No further income is anticipated in respect of the above estate. Accordingly, please find enclosed the final tax return in respect of the estate, together with the certificates of deduction of tax from your income. Please return the certificates to me in due course.

Please let me have a final tax assessment in respect of the estate.

I shall be obliged if you will also let me have (number required) forms R185E in respect of the beneficiaries.

Yours faithfully

Letter to capital tax office requesting inheritance tax clearance.

To: Capital taxes
Farrers House
PO Box 38
Castle Meadow Road
Nottingham
NG2 1BB

Dear Sir/Madam

Re: (Capital taxes reference, deceased details)

I would be grateful if you would let me have a formal inheritance tax clearance at your earliest convenience.

Yours faithfully

Letter to residuary beneficiaries enclosing accounts for approval

To: (name and address of beneficiary)

Dear

Re: the estate of (deceased)

The administration of the estate of the above has now been completed and I enclose copies of accounts in duplicate for your approval. Accounts have also been sent to the other parties fro their approval.

If you approve the accounts, please sign and date the form of discharge at the bottom of one copy and return that copy to me.

When all parties have returned the accounts to me approved I will be in a position to let you have a remittance for monies due to you.

If you have any queries please do not hesitate to contact me.

Yours faithfully

Appendix 2 – Example forms to be used in the process of probate

1. N205D-NOTICE OF ISSUE (PROBATE CLAIM)
2. PA1-HOW TO OBTAIN PROBATE
3. GUIDANCE NOTES FOR FORM PA1
4. APPLICATION FOR A PROBATE SEARCH
5. PA2-HOW TO OBTAIN PROBATE-GUIDE FOR THE APPLICANT WITHOUT SOLICITOR.
6. PROBATE FEES PA3
7. PROBATE REGISTRIES AND LOCAL INTERVIEW VENUES
8. MY PROBATE APPOINTMENT-WHAT HAPPENS NEXT?

Notice of issue
(probate claim)

In the

Claim No.

Claimant(s)

Click here to clear all fields

Defendant(s)

Issue fee

In the estate of   deceased (Probate)

Your claim was issued on [   ]

[The court sent it to the defendant(s) by first class post on [   ]

and it will be deemed served on [   ]].

[The claim form (which includes particulars of claim) is returned to you, with the relevant response forms, for

you to serve them on the defendant(s)]

Notes for guidance
The claim form and particulars of claim, if served separately, must be served on the defendant within 4 months
of the date of issue (6 months if you are serving outside England and Wales). You may be able to apply to
extend the time for serving the claim form but the application must generally be made before the 4 month or
6 month period expires.

You must inform the court immediately if your claim is settled.

The defendant must file an acknowledgment of service and defence within 28 days of service of the Particulars
of Claim (whether they are served with the claim form or separately). A longer period applies if the defendant
is served outside England and Wales.

Default judgment **cannot** be obtained in a probate claim.

If no defendant acknowledges service or files a defence, and the time for doing so has expired, you may apply to
the court for an order that the claim proceed to trial.

To

Ref.

N205D Notice of issue (probate) (10.01)

Probate Application Form - PA1

Please use **BLOCK CAPITALS**

Name of deceased

Interview venue _(see PA4)_

Dates to avoid

Please read the following questions and PA2 booklet 'How to obtain probate' carefully before filling in this form. Please also refer to the Guidance Notes PA1a where an item is marked *.

PLEASE COMPLETE ALL SECTIONS.

Section A: The Will / Codicil

This column is for official use

*A1	Did the deceased leave a will/codicil? _(Note: These may not necessarily be formal documents. If the answer to question 1 is Yes, you must enclose the **original** document(s) with your application.)_	**Will** Yes ☐ No ☐ **Codicil** Yes ☐ If **No** to both questions, please go to Section B

Date of will

Date of codicil

A2	Did the deceased marry or enter into a Civil Partnership after the date of the will/codicil?	Yes ☐ Date: No ☐
A3	Is there anyone under 18 years old who receives anything in the will/codicil?	Yes ☐ No ☐
A4	Did any of the witnesses to the will or codicil or the spouse/civil partner of any witness receive a gift under the will/codicil? If Yes, state name of witness.	Yes ☐ No ☐
A5	Are there any executors named in the will/codicil?	Yes ☐ No ☐
*A6	Give the names of those executors who are **not** applying and the reasons why. **Note: All executors must be accounted for.**	Full names — Reason A,B,C,D,E

A = Pre-deceased
B = Died after the deceased
C = Power Reserved
D = Renunciation
E = Power of Attorney

Section B: Relatives of the deceased

*B1 - B6

Please refer to the Guidance Notes.

Sections B1 - B4 must be completed in all cases.

Please state the **number** of relatives of the deceased in categories B1 - B4.

If there are no relatives in a particular category, write 'nil' in each box and move onto the next category.

Note: Sections B5 and B6 only need to be completed if the deceased had no relatives in Section B1 - B4.

Number of relatives (if none, write nil)	Under 18	Over 18
B1 Surviving **lawful** husband or wife or surviving **lawful** civil partner		
B2a Sons or daughters who survived the deceased		
b Sons or daughters who did **not** survive the deceased		
c Children of person(s) indicated at '2b' **only**, who survived the deceased *		
B3 Parents who survived the deceased		
B4a Brothers or sisters who survived the deceased		
b Brothers or sisters who did **not** survive the deceased		
c Children of person(s) indicated at '4b' **only**, who survived the deceased *		
B5 Grandparents who survived the deceased		
B6a Uncles or aunts who survived the deceased		
b Uncles or aunts who did **not** survive the deceased		
c Children of person(s) indicated at '6b' **only**, who survived the deceased *		

Please note that the grant will normally be sent to the first applicant. Any applicant named will be required to attend an interview. It is, however, usually only necessary for one person to apply (please see PA2 booklet, page 3).

This column is for official use

C1	Title	Mr ☐ Mrs ☐ Miss ☐ Ms ☐ Other ☐
C2	Forenames	
C3	Surname	
C4	Address	

I.T.W.C

Postcode:

C5	Telephone number

Home

Work

E-mail address (optional)

C6	Occupation

C7 Are you related to the deceased? Yes ☐ No ☐

If Yes, what is your relationship? Relationship:

C8 If there are any other applicants, up to a maximum of three, give their details. (Note: **All** applicants named in Sections C1 and C8 must attend an interview.)

Please give details below as C1 to C7 of other applicants who are entitled to apply and wish to be named in the grant.

C9 Name and address of any surviving lawful husband or wife/civil partner of the deceased, unless stated above.

Postcode:

*C10 If you are applying as an attorney on behalf of the person entitled to the grant, please state their name, address and capacity in which they are entitled (e.g. relationship to the deceased).

Postcode:

Relationship:

*C10a Has anyone been appointed by the person entitled as their attorney under an Enduring Power of Attorney (EPA) or a Property and financial affairs Lasting Power of Attorney (LPA)?

EPA ☐ LPA ☐ No ☐

*C10b If Yes, has it been registered with the Office of the Public Guardian?

Yes ☐ No ☐

*C10c Does the donor of the EPA/LPA lack mental capacity within the meaning of the Mental Capacity Act 2005? *(see PA1a)*

Yes ☐ No ☐

*D1   Forenames

*D2   Surname

True name

*D3   Did the deceased hold any assets **(excluding joint assets)** in another name?

Yes ☐   No ☐

Alias

*D4a   If Yes, what are the assets?

And in what name(s) are they held?

Address

D4b   Was the deceased known by any other name in which he/she made a will? If so, what name was it made in?

Yes ☐   No ☐

D5   Last permanent address of the deceased.

D/C district and No.

Postcode:

D6   Date of birth

D7   Date of death   Age:

L.S.A.

Domicile

D.B.F.

*D8   Was England and Wales the domicile/ permanent home of the deceased at the date of death? If No, please specify the deceased's permanent home or domicile.

Yes ☐   No ☐

*D9   Tick the last **legal** marital or civil partnership status of the deceased, and give dates where appropriate.

Bachelor/Spinster ☐

Widow/Widower/Surviving Civil Partner ☐

Married/Civil Partnership ☐   Date:

Divorced/Civil Partnership dissolved ☐   Date:

Judicially separated ☐   Date:

Note: These documents (♦) may usually be obtained from the Court which processed the divorce/dissolution of civil partnership/separation.

*(If the deceased did **not** leave a will, please enclose official copy♦ of the Decree Absolute/Decree of Dissolution of Civil Partnership/Decree of Judicial Separation (as applicable))*

*D10   Was the deceased legally adopted?

Yes ☐   No ☐

*D11   Has any relative of the deceased been legally adopted? (If Yes, give name and relationship to deceased.)

Yes ☐   No ☐

Name:

Relationship:

D12   *Answer this section **only** if the deceased died **before 4th April 1988 or left a will or codicil dated before that date.***

D12a   Was the deceased illegitimate?

Yes ☐   No ☐

D12b   Did the deceased leave any illegitimate sons or daughters?

Yes ☐   No ☐

D12c   Did the deceased have any illegitimate sons or daughters who died leaving children of their own?

Yes ☐   No ☐

i) **Complete this section if you have filled in form IHT205 (2006)/IHT207. You must file the form IHT205 (2006)/IHT207 with your application.**

If you have filled in a version of the IHT205 (2006) or IHT205 dated before 1st January 2011 please ring the Helpline on 0845 30 20 900 for advice.

I/We confirm that I/we have filled in form IHT205 (2006)/IHT207 and I/we confirm that from the answers I/we have given on that form I am/we are not required to fill in form IHT400 for this estate and the estate qualifies as an excepted estate. (Delete as applicable)

If you have filled in form IHT205 (2006) –
Please transfer the following figures from form IHT205 (2006) onto this form:

Figure from box D £
Figure from box F £
Figure from box H £

If you have filled in form IHT207 –
Please transfer the following figures from form IHT207 onto this form:

Figure from box A £
Figure from box C £
Figure from box H £

ii) **Complete this section if you have filled in form IHT400 and IHT421.**

Please transfer the following figures from form IHT421 on to this form:

Gross value of assets (from Box 3 on the IHT421) £
Net value (from Box 5 on the IHT421) £

At the same time as sending the probate application forms to the probate registry you **must** also send the **IHT400** (and associated schedules and copy documents) and **IHT421** to:

HMRC, Inheritance Tax, Ferrers House, PO Box 38, Castle Meadow Road, Nottingham, NG2 1BB (DX701201 Nottingham 4)

When the tax has been paid or assessed to be an estate where tax is not payable HMRC will send the stamped IHT421 to the appropriate probate registry as you have indicated on the IHT421 form.

Please send your application to the probate registry which controls the interview venue you wish to attend (see PA4) otherwise your application may be delayed.

You should send the following documents as applicable:

PA1

IHT205 (2006)/IHT207/IHT217 signed by all applicants (see Section E i)
Note: Do not enclose IHT400 or IHT421 – these must be sent to HMRC (Inheritance Tax) (see Section E ii)

Original will and codicils plus two A4 sized photocopies of the will/codicil(s) (see separate notes)
Note: Do not remove or attach anything to the will/codicil

An official copy of any foreign will or any will dealing with assets abroad (and a translation if necessary)

Official copy of death certificate or coroner's letter – **not a photocopy**

Other documents as requested on PA1

Please state the number of official copy grants required to deal with assets **in** England and Wales (see PA3)

Please state the number of official copy grants required to deal with assets **outside** England and Wales (see PA3)

Please state total amount of cheque enclosed for fee (made payable to **HM Courts & Tribunals Service**) including cost for the number of official copy grants stated above (see PA3) £

Dated

PLEASE ENSURE THAT ALL THE INFORMATION GIVEN IS ACCURATE AND THAT YOU KEEP COPIES OF ALL DOCUMENTS SENT. IF YOU DO NOT ENCLOSE ALL THE RELEVANT ITEMS YOUR APPLICATION MAY BE DELAYED.

Guidance Notes
for Probate Application Form PA1

These notes will help you to complete the parts of form PA1 marked * .

A1 Please enclose the original will and any codicils with your application (**not** a photocopy).

A6 Please state the names of any executors named in the will who are not applying for the Grant of Probate and show one of the following reasons for this:-

A   The executor died before the deceased.

B   The executor died after the deceased.

C   The executor does not wish to apply for probate now but wishes to reserve the right to act as executor in the future if necessary – this option is referred to as having "power reserved".

D   The executor does not wish to apply for probate at all. This is referred to as "renouncing". It means that they gives up all their rights to act as executor.

E   The executor wants to appoint another person to act as their attorney to take the Grant of Representation out on their behalf. Please note, however, that the attorney of one executor cannot take a grant jointly with an executor acting in his own right.

If you give reason D or E, please send a letter signed by the executor stating their intention when you send the application to the Probate Registry. If option C, D, or E is stated the Probate Registry will, on receipt of your application, send you a form for the executor(s) to sign to confirm their intention. You should arrange for this to be completed and then return it to the Probate Registry as instructed.

Example for A6

A will appoints three executors – Brian Jones, Valerie Jones and Frank Smith. Brian Jones wishes to apply for the grant, Frank Smith dies before the deceased and Valerie Jones does not wish to apply for the grant at present, as she works full time and cannot attend the appointment. Valerie wishes to keep her options open however, just in case it becomes necessary for her to take out a Grant of Probate in future e.g. if Brian Jones dies before he has completed the administration. The form would be completed as follows:

Frank Smith	A
Valerie Jones	C

The Grant of Probate will issue to Brian Jones with "power reserved" to Valerie Jones. Valerie Jones will be asked to sign a "power reserved" form.

Sections B1 - B4 must be completed in all cases. Sections B5 - B6 only needs to be completed if the deceased had no relatives in Sections B1 - B4.

Note:

- This section refers to blood/legally adopted relatives only; details of step relatives are not required.
- The term "survived" means the person was alive when the deceased died.
- If the deceased had any half brothers or sisters/uncles/aunts (i.e. only one parent in common), please indicate this on the form.
- A civil partnership is defined as one between two people of the same sex which has been registered in accordance with the Civil Partnership Act 2004.

B2(c), B4(c) and B6(c)

B2(c) – Only include children of sons or daughters of the deceased entered in B2(b), where the children have survived the deceased.

B4(c) – Only include children of brothers or sisters of the deceased entered in B4(b), where the children have survived the deceased.

B6(c) – Only include children of uncles or aunts of the deceased entered in B6(b), where the children have survived the deceased.

If you are applying on behalf of the person entitled to the grant (i.e. as their attorney), you should send a letter signed by them confirming that they want you to apply with your application. If the person entitled to the grant has already signed an Enduring Power of Attorney (EPA), or a Property and financial affairs Lasting Power of Attorney (LPA) please send the original document to us. An LPA must be registered with the Office of the Public Guardian before it can be used. If the donor of the EPA or LPA is unable to make a decision for him/herself due to an impairment of or a disturbance in the functioning of the mind or brain (i.e. lacks capacity under the Mental Capacity Act (MCA) 2005) please contact us.

D1 - D2   Please state the full **true** name of the deceased. The true name usually consists of the forenames as shown on the person's birth certificate and the surname as shown on the death certificate. If this is not the case please contact us.

D3 - D4   If the deceased had any assets in any name(s) other than their true name these should be stated. You do not need to show here any assets held jointly with another person.

Example for D1 - D4:

Name on birth certificate	Emma Louise **Jones**
Name on death certificate	Emma Louise **Smith**

The deceased's true name is Emma Louise Smith.

The deceased had a bank account in the name of Louise Smith and was commonly known by this name. The form should be completed as follows:

Forenames	**Emma Louise**
Surname	Smith
Did the deceased hold any assets (excluding joint assets) in another name?	Yes
If yes, what are the assets?	Lloyds Bank Account
And in what name(s) are they held?	**Louise** Smith

The grant will issue in the name of "Emma Louise Smith otherwise known as Louise Smith".

D8   The domicile of the deceased at the date of their death must be established in each case. Generally a person is domiciled in the country which they consider to be their permanent home. However they may be domiciled in a country without having a permanent home there. If you are unsure what this means you should contact your local registry. You may need to seek legal advice regarding this.

D9   You do not initially need to supply a copy of the Decree Absolute, decree of dissolution of civil partnership or decree of Judicial Separation if the deceased left a will. However we may ask to see it later if necessary. You can obtain an official copy of these documents from the court that issued them or from Principal Registry of the Family Division, 42-49 High Holborn, London WC1V 6NP.

D10 - D11   If the deceased did **not** leave a will and the applicant for the grant is the adoptor/adoptee of the deceased, please file a copy of the entry in the Adopted Children's Register. An official copy of the entry in the Adopted Children's Register can be obtained from The General Register Office, Adoption Section, Smedley Hydro, Trafalgar Road, Birkdale, Southport PR8 2HH.

If you have any general enquiries,
please telephone the Probate and Inheritance Tax Helpline
Telephone number: 0845 3020900

Application for a probate search

When completing your form please use CAPITAL LETTERS

Details of the Deceased

Surname

Forenames

Probate details (if known)

Grant type: Issuing Registry: Grant issue date:

Date of death/search period*

Address

* (see Conditions of Service
on next page)

Document requirements/payment

Do you want a copy of the Will (if any)?   Yes [ ]   No [ ]   If Yes, how many? [ ]

Do you want a copy of the Grant of Probate
or Letters of Administration (if any)?   Yes [ ]   No [ ]   If Yes, how many? [ ]

I enclose a crossed cheque/Postal Order
(payable to HM Courts Service) to the value of   (see notes on fees
on next page)   £

Your own details

Name/Organisation

Your ref. (if any)

Address/DX number and
Exchange

Please send the completed form, together with your payment, by post to: The Postal Searches and Copies
Department, The Probate Registry, Castle Chambers, Clifford Street, York YO1 9RG (DX720629 York 21)

For official use

Postal Searches and Copies Department:
Information and Conditions of Service

Applicable dates and records held: The Postal Searches and Copies Department has indexes relating to all Probate records for the whole of England and Wales from 11 January 1858 up to the present day. You may apply for a copy of any proved Will, as well as a copy of the Grant of Representation. The Grant will tell you who were the Executors or Administrators (those appointed to gather in and distribute the estate). It may also tell you the name of the Solicitor acting for them (if any) and the value of the estate, although usually only in very broad terms. The financial summary shown on the Grant is unfortunately the only information relating to the estate that the Probate record contains. No inventory or estate accounts are available. Occasionally, further details are available from the Capital Taxes Office, but you will normally need the written consent of the executors or administrators. **Please note that, if Probate has not been granted, the Probate Service will have no record of the estate and will therefore not be able to provide copies of any document relating to it.**

If the death was recent, it may be that Probate has not yet been cleared. The Probate procedure itself normally takes some weeks, and there may have been a considerable further delay before the application for Probate was made. Consequently, it may be advisable to wait two or three months after the date of death before having a search made, in order to allow time for the Probate process to be completed.

If you apply before Probate has been completed, you will be notified that no details are available. If you wish to pursue your enquiry, you will need to reapply after a suitable interval, enclosing a further fee and resubmitting all the relevant details, or enter a Standing Search. A Standing Search remains in force for a period of 6 months from the date of entry and provides copies of the Will (if any) and Grant if a Grant issues during this period. Contact the Postal Searches and Copies Department or any Probate Registry for further details.

Other parts of the UK and the Republic of Ireland: The jurisdiction of the Probate Service is limited to England and Wales. If the deceased died domiciled in Scotland, you could try contacting HM Commissary Office, 27 Chambers Street, Edinburgh EH1 2NS (Tel: 0131 247 2850) if the death occurred after 1985, or the Scottish Records Office, HM General Register House, Edinburgh EH1 3YY (Tel: 0131 535 1334) for records prior to this. For Northern Ireland, contact the Probate and Matrimonial Office, The Royal Courts of Justice, Belfast BT1 3JF (Tel: 028 9023 5111), or, if the death occurred more than 7 years ago, the Public Record Office of Northern Ireland, 66 Balmoral Street, Belfast, BT9 6NY (Tel: 028 9025 1318). For the Republic of Ireland, contact the Probate Office, Fourt Courts, Dublin 7 (Tel: Dublin 725555), or the National Archives Office, Bishop Street, Dublin 8 (Tel: Dublin 407 2300) for records more than 20 years old. The Channel Islands and the Isle of Man also have independent Probate Courts.

Fees: When returning the completed application to the Postal Searches and Copies Department in York, please also enclose the fee of £5.00. Each **extra copy** of the same document ordered at the same time will attract an additional fee of £1.00. Cheques or Postal Orders should be crossed and made payable to 'HM Courts Service'. Fees from abroad should be paid by International Money Order, cheque or draft, payable through a United Kingdom bank, and must be made out in £ sterling. We are currently unable to accept payments by credit or debit card, nor are we able to receive search requests by telephone. Please contact the Postal Searches and Copies Department for details of fees for special copies (for instance if you are administering estate abroad), and mark your application accordingly.

The standard fee covers a 4-year search starting from the year in which the death occurred (or the year from which you ask us to start searching). Longer searches are charged at a rate of £3.00 per 4-year period, so that an 8-year search will cost £8.00, and a 12-year search £11.00. Please specify the period to be searched (as well as the date of death if known) and send the appropriate fee. If the death occurred within the last 4 years, the search will be made up to the most recent index. If the search is successful, we will obtain and forward copies of the Will and/or Grant as requested. If no Grant has issued in this time, you will be notified accordingly. We aim to respond to your request within 21 working days.

If a record is traced, the standard fee includes one copy of the Will, if any, and Grant, if requested. Please state clearly which document(s) you require. If the details you supply are incomplete, ambiguous or incorrect and the documents cannot be traced as a result, you will be asked to reapply, giving the correct information and enclosing a further payment. We cannot accept responsibility for the accuracy of the search unless full and correct details are given that accord with the information supplied on application for the Grant, normally the information in the Register of Deaths. If there is insufficient information to make a search, we will contact you for further details. **Please note that your payment is not refundable in the event of a negative search result.**

Original documents: If you are applying for copies of older documents, you should be aware that some of these are in poor condition. Although we make every effort to produce a legible copy from the documents we hold, a small proportion will be of unavoidable poor quality. Furthermore, copies are normally made from the record copies held by the Probate Service. This means that documents prior to the early 1930s will be, by default, copies of manuscript or typescript record copies, and not facsimile copies of the original document. If you want facsimile copies of the original, you will need to mark your request very clearly to that effect.

PA2

How to obtain probate -

A guide for people acting without a solicitor

What is the Probate Service?

The Probate Service is part of HM Courts & Tribunals Service. It administers the system of probate, which gives people the legal right to handle the estate (for example, money, possessions and property) of a deceased person.

This leaflet will advise you if you want to obtain probate without using a solicitor.

If you have any queries, please contact your local probate registry. The staff are there to help you – but please note that they cannot give you legal advice.

Introduction

When a person dies, they usually leave an estate (including money, possessions and property) and sometimes a will.

A will should name one or more executors who are responsible for collecting in all the money, paying any debts and distributing any legacies left to individuals or organisations.

In order to access the estate, the executor needs to apply to the probate registry for a document called a Grant of Representation or 'grant'. This process is called probate. The grant establishes who can legally collect money from banks, building societies and other organisations which hold assets belonging to the deceased person.

In most cases, applying for probate is a straightforward procedure. The Probate Service administers applications for grants throughout England and Wales.

The information in this leaflet refers only to the law in England and Wales. If the deceased person was permanently resident in Scotland, Northern Ireland or another country when they died, please contact your nearest probate registry for advice.

What is the purpose of the Grant of Representation?

A Grant of Representation establishes who can legally collect money from banks, building societies and other organisations that hold assets belonging to the deceased person. There are three types of Grant of Representation:

Probate

Probate is issued by the Probate Service to the executor(s) named in the deceased person's will.

Letters of Administration (with will)

Letters of Administration (with will) are issued when no executor is named in the will, or when the executors are unable or unwilling to apply for the grant.

Letters of Administration

Letters of Administration are issued when the deceased person has not made a will, or the will they have made is not valid.

Is a grant always needed?

Not every estate needs a grant. A grant may not be needed if:

- the home is held in joint names and is passing by survivorship to the other joint owner(s). This can be the case for married couples and those in a legal civil partnership.
- there is a joint bank or building society account. In this case, the bank may only need to see the death certificate, in order to arrange for the money to be transferred to the other joint owner. However, a grant could still be needed to access assets held in other bank accounts or insurance policies.
- the amount held in each account was very small. You will need to check with the organisations (banks, building societies or insurance companies) involved to find out if they will release the assets without a grant.

If none of the circumstances above apply, a grant may be required.

You should ask anyone holding the deceased's money (such as a bank or insurance company) whether they will release it to you without seeing a grant. If they agree, they may attach conditions such as asking you to sign a statutory declaration before a solicitor. You can decide whether it is cheaper or easier to do this than to apply for a grant.

Please note that a grant **must** be presented in order to sell or transfer a property held in the deceased's sole name or a share of a property held jointly with the deceased person's spouse or partner as tenants-in-common. Tenancy-in-common is a written agreement between two people who own a joint asset (usually land or buildings). Normally, a married couple does not have a tenancy-in-common contract. If you aren't sure about this, you should consult a solicitor.

You cannot complete a sale on any property owned by a deceased person until the grant has been issued. Properties named in a will should not be put up for sale until a grant has been obtained.

Who can apply for probate?

It isn't necessary for everyone left money or property in a will to apply for probate. Usually, only one person needs to do it – normally the executor(s) named in the will.

However, if the person entitled to the estate is under 18, two people are legally required to apply for probate. If this is the case we will let you know when we receive your application.

You can apply for probate if you are over the age of 18 and:

- you are an executor named in the will;
- you are named in the will to receive some or all of the estate (if there are no executors, or if the executors are unable or unwilling to apply);

- the deceased person did not make a will and you are their next of kin, in the following order of priority:

  - lawful husband or wife or civil partner (a civil partnership is defined as a partnership between two people of the same sex which has been registered in accordance with the Civil Partnership Act 2004). Common law partners cannot apply for probate.

  - sons or daughters (excluding step-children) including children adopted by the deceased. (Children adopted out of the family can only apply in the estates of their adoptive parents and not their biological parents.)

  - parents

  - brothers or sisters

  - grandparents

  - uncles or aunts

  - If sons, daughters, brothers, sisters, uncles or aunts of the deceased person have died before the deceased, their children may apply for probate.

If you are not sure whether you are entitled to apply for a grant, you should still complete and return the forms and we will tell you. If you are a distant relative, please supply a brief family tree showing your relationship to the deceased person.

When more than one person wants to apply for a grant, they may make a joint application. A maximum of four applicants is allowed and they will all have to attend an interview with the Probate Service.

Where will I find the will?

The original will may be held at a solicitor's office or bank, or at the Principal Probate Registry in London. It may be among the deceased person's possessions. If you cannot find it, contact your local Probate Registry. If you do not send the will, your application will take longer to deal with.

We will not return the original will to you as it becomes a public record once it has been proved (acted on). We will, however, send you an official copy of the will with the Grant of Representation.

What if I don't want to apply for a grant?

Executors may choose to give up all their rights to probate or they may reserve the right, called power reserved, to apply for probate in the future.

This option is often used when the executors live in different parts of the country or it is not convenient for one of them to attend the interview due to work commitments.

Only the executor(s) who attend the interview will be named on the grant and only their signature will be required to release the deceased person's assets for transfer or sale.

If the person who is entitled to the grant does not wish to apply, they may appoint someone else to be their attorney to obtain the grant on their behalf. If this is the case you should complete their details on form **PA1** (Section C). We will send you a form for them to sign after we receive your application. If the person entitled to the grant has already signed an Enduring Power of Attorney (EPA) or a Lasting Power of Attorney (LPA) please file the original document with your application.

Note – A LPA must be registered with the Office of the Public Guardianship before it can be used.

You can contact them via www.publicguardian.gov.uk or by calling 0845 330 2900.

Why do I need to think about Inheritance Tax now?

The tax on the estate of a person who has died is called Inheritance Tax. It is dealt with by HM Revenue & Customs (HMRC) (Inheritance Tax). It only applies to a very small percentage of estates. If Inheritance Tax is due, you normally have to pay at least some of the tax before we can issue the grant.

The issue of the grant does not mean that HMRC (Inheritance Tax) have agreed the final Inheritance Tax liability. They will usually contact you again after you have received the grant. Subject to the requirements to pay some of the tax before obtaining the grant, Inheritance Tax is due six months after the end of the month in which the person died. HMRC (Inheritance Tax) will charge interest on unpaid tax from this due date whatever the reason for late payment.

Probate Registry staff are not trained to deal with queries about HMRC forms or Inheritance Tax. If you have any queries about these you should visit the HMRC website: www.hmrc.gov.uk/inheritancetax or contact the Probate and Inheritance Tax Helpline on 0845 30 20 900.

How do I apply for a grant?

You will need to follow the process explained here:

Complete the application form

You will need to complete **Probate Application form PA1, using Guidance Leaflet PA1A**. You can also get these forms from your nearest probate registry or by calling the Probate and Inheritance Tax Helpline – see page 7 for details.

These documents are also available online at hmctsformfinder.justice.gov.uk. You should print off a blank **PA1** and then complete it by hand.

On the application form, you should tell us which Probate Registry interview venue you would like to visit – you can choose the one which is most convenient for you, and any other executors.

Complete the tax form

When you apply for the grant, you will need to complete a tax form **whether or not Inheritance Tax is owed**. You should use form **IHT205** if no Inheritance Tax is owed. If form **IHT205** is not applicable to you, please contact HMRC (Inheritance Tax) for form **IHT400**.

For help completing the forms, you can contact the Probate and Inheritance Tax Helpline (the phone number is on page 7 of this leaflet). You can either work out the Inheritance Tax for yourself or you can ask HMRC to do it for you.

Decide how many official sealed copies of the Grant of Representation you need

Organisations like banks and building societies need to see sealed copies of the grant before they can release assets to you. They won't accept unsealed photocopies.

So if you want to deal with the estate quickly, you may want to order enough sealed copies of the grant to send to all the organisations you are dealing with at the same time.

If there are any assets held outside England and Wales, you may require a special copy of the grant – usually referred to as a sealed and certified copy.

If any person or organisation holding assets insists on seeing an official copy of the grant, you can write to the probate registry, which issued the grant to order more sealed copies. However, these will cost more than those ordered at the time of application (see the fee list), so it's important to decide before you apply for the grant how many copies you will need.

Make sure you enclose the correct documents

You will need to enclose:

- An official copy (**not** a photocopy) of the death certificate issued by the Registrar of Births Deaths and Marriages or a coroner's certificate.

- The **original** will and any codicils (or any document in which the deceased person expresses any wishes about the distribution of his or her estate). Keep a copy of any will or codicil you send us. Please do not attach anything to the will by staple, pin etc. or remove any fastenings from the will.

- Any other documents specifically requested by the Probate Service, such as a decree absolute.

- A cheque made payable to 'HM Courts & Tribunals Service' for the application fee, together with the cost of the number of official sealed grants you require. See the fees list on form **PA3**. (We cannot process your application until the fee has been paid.)

Where should I send my application?

You should send your application to the probate registry of your choice (see leaflet **PA4** for the address). You may wish to send your application by registered or recorded post.

Processing the application

When we receive your application, we will examine it and contact you if there are any queries. If you want us to acknowledge your application, please send a stamped addressed envelope.

If your application is complicated, we may require you to sign additional documents or contact other people – for example, a witness to a will – so that we can interview them or obtain their signatures on documents to help with your application.

If there are no problems, we will send you a letter (usually ten days after we receive your application) inviting you to a 10-15 minute interview at the location you have chosen. This interview is usually held within a month of receiving your application.

If you are applying for a grant with someone else and they cannot come with you, we can arrange for them to attend an interview separately at a different location if necessary. This will, however, delay the time it takes to issue your grant.

What happens at the interview?

The interview is simply to confirm the details you have given on the forms and to answer any queries you or we may have.

We also ask you to sign a form of oath and to swear or affirm before the interviewing officer that the information you have given is true to the best of your knowledge. You will be given the opportunity to swear on the religious book of your choice.

Please bring proof of identification which includes a photograph (such as your driving licence or passport) to the interview. Your appointment letter will tell you about any other identification which is required.

The interview is your chance to tell the interviewing officer if your case is urgent or if you wish to collect the grant in person.

What happens after the interview?

If everything goes smoothly, we will send you the original grant and copies of the grant (if you have requested them) and the original death certificate. The interviewing officer should be able to let you know how long this will take.

If it is not possible to issue a grant, we will explain the reasons.

We retain the original will, as it becomes a public record.

How do I use the grant?

When the grant has been issued you will receive information concerning your role as the executor. You will then have the legal right to ask any person or organisation holding the deceased person's money or property to give you access to these assets. These assets can then be released, sold or transferred as set out in the deceased person's will.

All grants of representation are public records.

The responsibility of the Probate Service ends when the grant is issued, and we cannot advise you on how to administer the estate. If you have any questions about this, you should seek legal advice.

Useful contacts

For general information on wills and probate:
www.direct.gov.uk/death

To access the online forms and leaflets:
hmctsformfinder.justice.gov.uk

To find the addresses of the regional probate registries:
hmctscourtfinder.justice.gov.uk

For information about Inheritance Tax and online forms:
www.hmrc.gov.uk/inheritancetax

For more detailed information about probate and Inheritance Tax:
Probate and Inheritance Tax Helpline: 0845 3020900

Probate forms and leaflets

PA1   Probate application form
PA1A   Probate application form (guidance notes)
PA2   How to obtain probate (leaflet)
PA3   Probate fees list (leaflet)
PA4   Directory of probate registries and interview venues (leaflet)
PA5   Do I need a grant of representation (probate or letters of administration)? (leaflet)
PA6   What will happen at my probate interview? (leaflet)
PA7   How to deposit a will with the Probate Service (leaflet)
PA7A   Withdrawing your will from the Principal Probate Registry (form)
PA8   How to enter a caveat (leaflet)
PA8A   How to enter a caveat (form)
PA9   How to enter a general search (leaflet)
PA10   How to enter a standing search (leaflet)
PA1S   Application for a probate search (form)

HMRC Inheritance Tax forms

IHT205 Return of estate information
IHT206 Return of estate information (guidance notes)
IHT400 Inheritance Tax Account

HM Courts & Tribunals Service

PA3

Probate Fees from April 2011

	Fee
Application In all cases where the net estate (ie the amount remaining in the deceased's sole name after funeral expenses and debts owing have been deducted) is **over £5,000** (see example 1 below). **Note: Joint assets passing automatically to the surviving joint owner should not be included when calculating the fee.**	£105
If the net estate as above is **under £5,000** (see example 2 below).	No fee
Application for a second grant in an estate where a previous grant has been issued.	£20
Additional Copies Official (sealed) copies of the Grant of Representation if ordered when you lodge your application for a Grant of Representation. **Note: You should decide how many copies you will need and add the cost to your application fee – this will give you the total amount payable. See examples below. It can save you a lot of time when collecting in the deceased's assets if you have a few extra copies of the grant to produce to the organisations holding the assets.**	£1 per copy
'Sealed and certified copy' – if assets are held abroad you may need one of these. Please check with the appropriate organisations before ordering.	£1 per copy (including Will and Grant)
Additional copies (consisting of grant including a copy of the Will, if applicable) ordered after the Grant of Representation has been issued.	£6 for first copy then £1 per additional copy

Example 1				**Example 2**			
Net estate of £75,000	=	Fee	£105	Net estate of £2,000	=	Fee	Nil
4 copies of grant at £1	=	Fee	£ 4	1 copy of grant at £1	=	Fee	£1
each		Total Fee	£109	each		Total Fee	£1

Please send a cheque or postal order (no cash) made payable to '**HM Courts & Tribunals Service**', together with your application forms, to the Probate Registry to which you are applying. You should state the number and type of copies you need on the checklist on page 4 of the PA1 (application form). Please print the name of the **deceased person** on the back of the cheque.

Please ensure you order sufficient copies for your needs, when you send in your application.

Please note: Appropriate post must be paid. (Standard rate postage may not be sufficient. If your forms weigh over 60g they may need to be weighed at your local Post Office.)

What if I cannot afford to pay a fee?

If you cannot afford the fee, you may be eligible for a fee remission in full or part. The combined booklet and application form EX160A - Court fees - do I have to pay them? gives all the information you need. You can get a copy from any Probate Registry or from our website www.hmcourts-service.gov.uk.

Your application will not be processed until the fee is paid (or an application for refund/remission has been successful).

Directory of Probate Registries and Interview Venues

> For general enquiries, please telephone the Probate & Inheritance Tax Help-line Monday to Friday 9.00 to 5.00 on 0845 3020900.
>
> For enquiries about appointments, or for enquiries after you have sent your forms to a Probate Registry, please contact the Registry concerned, using the number listed below.

Controlling Probate Registries (except for Carlisle, Chester, Lancaster, Leicester, and Middlesbrough, Peterborough and York) are open to the public 9.30 am to 4.00 pm Monday to Friday. London is open from 10.00 am to 4.00 pm Monday to Friday.

You can choose any venue for your appointment to swear the oath, **but your application** *must* **be sent to the Controlling Probate Registry responsible for that venue.**

Most locations, other than Probate Registries, have limited opening times as there is limited demand in many locations. When selecting a venue your appointment will be fixed for the next available date. However, if there is no date fixed for the venue of your choice you will be given an appointment date at the main registry, as this will be much earlier. If, when you receive notification of the date and location, you want to change the location (or the date) you should telephone the controlling Registry (phone number will be supplied at that time) to see if an appointment can be made at another venue (although this may be at a much later date) or on another date.

Controlling Probate Registry	Interview Venues	Controlling Probate Registry	Interview Venues
Birmingham District Probate Registry The Priory Courts 33 Bull Street Birmingham B4 6DU Tel: 0121 681 3400/3414	Birmingham Coventry Kidderminster Northampton Wolverhampton	**Carlisle Probate Sub-Registry** Courts of Justice Earl Street, Carlisle CA1 1DJ Tel: 01228 521751	Carlisle
Bodmin Probate Sub-Registry Bodmin Magistrates Court Launceston Road Bodmin Cornwall PL31 2AL Tel: 01208 261581	Bodmin Plymouth Truro	**Carmarthen Probate Sub-Registry** 14 King Street Carmarthen SA31 1BL Tel: 01267 242560	Carmarthen Aberystwyth Haverfordwest Swansea
Brighton District Probate Registry William Street Brighton BN2 0RF Tel: 01273 573510	Brighton Chichester Hastings Horsham	**Chester Probate Sub-Registry** Please send applications to Liverpool District Probate Registry (see address on page 2)	
Bristol District Probate Registry The Civil Justice Centre 2 Redcliff Street Bristol BS1 6GR Tel: 0117 3664960/61	Bristol Bath Weston-Super-Mare	**Exeter Probate Sub-Registry** 1st Floor Exeter Crown & County Courts Southernhay Gardens Exeter, Devon EX1 1UH Tel: 01392 415370	Exeter Barnstaple Taunton Torquay/Newton Abbot Yeovil
Caernarfon Probate Sub-Registry The Criminal Justice Centre Llanberis Road Caernarfon LL55 2DF Tel: 01286 669 755	Caernarfon Rhyl Wrexham	**Gloucester Probate Sub-Registry** 2nd Floor, Combined Court Building Kimbrose Way Gloucester GL1 2DG Tel: 01452 834966	Gloucester Cheltenham Hereford Worcester
Cardiff Probate Registry of Wales 3rd Floor, Cardiff Magistrates' Court Fitzalan Place, Cardiff South Wales CF24 0RZ Tel: 02920 474373	Cardiff Bridgend Newport Pontypridd	**Ipswich District Probate Registry** Ground Floor 8 Arcade Street Ipswich IP1 1EJ Tel: 01473 284260	Ipswich Chelmsford Colchester

Controlling Probate Registry	Interview Venues	Controlling Probate Registry	Interview Venues
Lancaster Probate Sub-Registry Please send applications to Liverpool District Probate Registry (see address below)		**Newcastle-Upon-Tyne District Probate Registry** Newcastle DPR No 1 Waterloo Square Newcastle-Upon-Tyne NE1 4DR Tel: 0191 211 2170	Newcastle-Upon-Tyne Darlington Middlesbrough
Leeds District Probate Registry York House York Place Leeds LS1 2BA Tel: 0113 3896 133	Leeds	**Norwich Probate Sub-Registry** Combined Court Building The Law Courts Bishopgate Norwich NR3 1UR Tel: 01603 728267	Norwich Kings Lynn Lowestoft
Leicester Probate Sub-Registry Crown Court Building 90 Wellington Street Leicester LE1 6HG Tel: 0116 285 3380	Leicester Bedford	**Nottingham Probate Sub-Registry** Butt Dyke House 33 Park Row Nottingham NG1 6GR Tel: 0115 941 4288	Nottingham
Lincoln Probate Sub-Registry 360 High Street Lincoln LN5 7PS Tel: 01522 523648	Lincoln	**Oxford District Probate Registry** Combined Court Building St Aldates Oxford OX1 1LY Tel: 01865 793055	Oxford Aylesbury High Wycombe Reading Slough Swindon
Liverpool District Probate Registry The Queen Elizabeth II Law Courts Derby Square Liverpool L2 1XA Tel: 0151 236 8264	Liverpool Southport Lancaster Blackpool Preston St Helens Chester	**Peterborough Probate Sub-Registry** 1st Floor, Crown Building Rivergate Peterborough PE1 1EJ Tel: 01733 562802	Peterborough Cambridge
London Probate Department Principal Registry of the Family Division First Avenue House 42-49 High Holborn London WC1V 6NP Tel: 020 7947 6939 Open 10.00am-4.30pm Mon-Fri	London Croydon Edmonton Kingston Luton Southend-on-Sea Woolwich	**Sheffield Probate Sub-Registry** PO Box 832 The Law Courts 50 West Bar Sheffield S3 8YR Tel: 0114 281 2596	Sheffield
Maidstone Probate Sub-Registry The Law Courts Barker Road Maidstone ME16 8EQ Tel: 01622 202048	Maidstone Canterbury Tunbridge Wells	**Stoke-on-Trent Probate Sub-Registry** Combined Court Centre Bethesda Street Hanley Stoke-on-Trent ST1 3BP Tel: 01782 854065	Stoke-on-Trent Stafford Shrewsbury Crewe
Manchester District Probate Registry Manchester Civil Justice Centre Ground Floor 1 Bridge Street West PO Box 4240 Manchester M60 1WJ Tel: 0161 240 5700	Manchester Bolton Burnley Oldham Warrington Wigan	**Winchester District Probate Registry** 4th Floor Cromwell House Andover Road Winchester SO23 7EW Tel: 01962 897029	Winchester Basingstoke Bournemouth Dorchester Guildford Newport I.O.W. Portsmouth Salisbury Southampton
Middlesbrough Probate Sub-Registry Please send applications to Newcastle District Probate Registry (see address opposite)		**York Probate Sub-Registry** Please send applications to Leeds District Probate Registry (see address opposite)	York Hull Scarborough

My probate appointment - What will happen?

Why do I need to come for an appointment?

The appointment is to confirm the information that you have sent us in your application, which will enable the Probate Service to issue a Grant of Representation. This grant will authorise you to deal with the estate of the deceased person. The appointment will also give you the opportunity to ask any questions you may have.

Where will the appointment take place?

The appointment will be held at the venue indicated on your appointment letter – if this is incorrect, please contact us. The appointment will be in a private room. You will not have to go into a courtroom.

Please follow the instructions on the reverse of your appointment letter and ensure you arrive 10 minutes before the time of the appointment so you do not cause delay to others.

Who is the appointment with?

The appointment will be informal and will be with a member of staff from the Probate Service, who is called a Commissioner. You will not have to see a judge.

How long will the appointment last?

The appointment should last no longer than 15 minutes.

What facilities are available?

Please see your letter of appointment for specific details. If you have any special needs, please contact the Registry to which you sent your application before the date of the appointment.

May I bring a friend or relative with me?

Yes, you are welcome to do so.

Do I need to bring any identification with me?

Yes – each personal applicant should bring with them to the interview two separate forms of identification from the following list:-

- Full driving licence
- Passport
- Official bus pass
- National insurance card or National Health card
- State pension notification letter
- Child benefit notification letter
- A letter or invoice showing your current address from a utilities company
- Community tax bill.

If you do not have any of the above, please contact us before your interview.

What else do I need to bring?

If we have asked you to bring any documents with you to the appointment, please don't forget them or your appointment may need to be re-arranged for another day. You do not need to bring any other documents such as bank statements etc.

If you wear glasses for reading please bring them.

What will happen at the appointment?

You will be asked to read through a document, referred to as 'The Oath', which we will have prepared from the information you have already given us in your application form.

You will then be asked to confirm that the information in that document is correct, to the best of your knowledge.

Next you will be asked to swear on the New Testament that the contents of The Oath are true.

If you do not want to swear on the New Testament you may either:-

- make an affirmation (which means to make a legal declaration) that the contents are true,

or

- swear on another religious book. If you wish to do this, please contact the office at the top of your appointment letter, before the day of your appointment.

Will I be given the grant at the appointment?

No. It will be posted to you, by second class post, usually within 10 working days of your appointment, together with any copies for which you have paid.

If form D18 has been filed, the grant, and copies, will be posted to you when the Capital Taxes Office has confirmed that it is satisfied the Grant of Representation can be issued.

Any queries regarding Inheritance Tax should be made to the Capital Taxes Office (Helpline – 0845 3020900) (calls charged at local rate).

Which documents will I get back?

The Death Certificate **will** be returned to you after the appointment.

The original Will of the deceased **will not** be returned to you. You will receive an official copy of the Will with the Grant of Representation. The original Will is kept by the Probate Registry and becomes part of public records.

Please note that we cannot give any legal advice about, for example, the distribution of an estate. You may need to speak to a solicitor/legal adviser or visit a Citizens Advice Bureau.

Page 3

PA6 My probate appointment - what will happen? (02.06)

HMCS

Index